Student Study Guide

to accompany

Fundamentals of
Early Childhood Education

Third Edition

George S. Morrison
University of North Texas

Prepared by
Mary Nelle Brunson
Stephen F. Austin State University

Merrill
Prentice Hall

Upper Saddle River, New Jersey
Columbus, Ohio

10 9 8 7 6 5 4 3 2 1

Merrill
Prentice Hall

ISBN: 0-13-048642-6

Contents of the Student Study Guide

The *Student Study Guide* is designed as a self-guided tool to assist you with the acquisition of text knowledge. The study guide will lead you through each chapter and assist you with identifying the important knowledge base for the early childhood professional. Each chapter contains the objectives, an overview, a study guide, a technology tie-in and a self-check quiz.

I.   Chapter Objectives

The learner outcomes for each chapter are stated to help you identify the learning expectations for the chapter.

II.   Chapter Preview

Key concepts are presented in the overview that corresponds to the major headings in the chapters of the textbook.

III.   Study Guide

The study guide outlines the chapter and asks you to respond to questions that relate to the major headings of the textbook. Key terms found in the chapter are included in the study guide. Charts help you focus on key concepts presented in the chapter.

IV.   Technology Tie-In

Each chapter of the study guide contains a technology tie-in to help enhance your knowledge about technology as well as the major topics in the chapter. The technology activities will help you make connections between the information in the chapter and the application of that information to classroom practice. The activities will support your development as an early childhood professional and assist you with the collection of information to support your future career.

V.   Self Check

A sample quiz is included to provide you with an opportunity to check your knowledge of the content of each chapter. Questions on the quiz are similar to those provided in the Test Bank of the *Instructor's Manual*. Essay questions are included to guide your understanding of the material presented. Answers for the Self-Check are provided at the end of the *Student Study Guide*.

TABLE OF CONTENTS

CHAPTER 1

YOU AND EARLY CHILDHOOD EDUCATION: WHAT DOES IT MEAN TO BE A PROFESSIONAL?

I. Chapter Objectives

Learner outcomes:
The learner will:

- describe the early childhood professional;

- explain the dimensions of the early childhood professional;

- define the terminology of early childhood education.

II. Chapter Overview

Who is an early childhood professional?

What can you do to demonstrate the personal dimensions of professionalism?

What can you do to demonstrate the educational dimensions of professionalism?

What can you do to demonstrate the practice of professionalism?

What can you do to demonstrate the public dimensions of professionalism?

III. <u>Chapter 1 Study Guide</u>
Text pages 2-27.

Directions: As you read the chapter, answer the following questions. Use the guide to study the chapter information.

Who is an Early Childhood Professional?

1.   Define the term early childhood professional.

_____

_____

_____

_____

The Four Dimensions of Professionalism

2.   Identify and explain the four dimensions of a high-quality early childhood professional.

Dimensions of Professionalism

Personal characteristics
- Personal character

- Emotional qualities

- Physical health

- Mental health

Professional practice

- Knowing children

- Developmentally and culturally appropriate practice

- Planning

- Assessing

- Reporting

- Reflecting and thinking

- Teaching

- Collaborating with parents, families, and community partners

- Engaging in ethical practice

- Seeking ongoing professional development opportunities

- Advocacy

- Articulation

- Representation

---

3. A philosophy of education is a set of beliefs about how children develop and learn and what and how they should be taught (see page 13 in text).

   Read Linda Luna DeMino's Philosophy on Early Childhood Education.

   Write your beliefs about children and learning.

   _____

   _____

   _____

   _____

   _____

   Use your belief statements to complete the following:
   I believe the purposes of education are ...

   _____

   _____

   _____

   _____

   _____

I believe that children learn best when ...

_____

_____

_____

_____

_____

The curriculum of any classroom should include certain "basics" that contribute to children's social, emotional, intellectual, and physical development. These basics are ...

_____

_____

_____

_____

Children learn best in an environment that promotes learning. Features of a good learning environment are...

_____

_____

_____

_____

All children have certain needs that must be met if they are to grow and learn at their best. Some of these basic needs are ...

_____

_____

_____

_____

I would meet these needs by ...

_____

_____

_____

_____

A teacher should have certain qualities. Qualities I think important for
teaching are...

_____

_____

_____

_____

Now rewrite your statements to create your first draft of your philosophy of
education.

Using the Professional Development Checklist

4.   Refer to Figure 1.3 in the text and review the Thirteen Steps to Becoming a
        Professional: A Development Checklist. After reviewing Figure 1.3 and reading the
        text, identify four or more things you will do this semester to help prepare for a
        career in early childhood education. List the four you selected and your plan to
        accomplish your goals.

_____

_____

_____

_____

What is the Terminology of Early Childhood Education?

5.   Define each of the following:

professional _____

_____

caregiver _____

_____

teacher _____

_____

early childhood _____

_____

early childhood program _____

_____

early childhood education _____

_____

preschool _____

_____

prekindergarten _____

_____

kindergarten _____

_____

junior first or pre-first grade _____

_____

preprimary _____

_____

child care _____

_____

family day care _____

_____

Head Start _____

_____

Follow Through _____

_____

Early Head Start _____

_____

IV. <u>Technology Tie-In</u>

Making Connections

After you have assessed your technology competency, go to the Internet4Classrooms web site and complete an on-line practice module that will help you develop the competencies you need to be technologically proficient. Use the list of technology tutorials found on-line to help you design your technology development plan.

Internet4Classrooms On-Line Practice Modules
http://www.internet4classrooms.com/on-line.htm

Internet Log

Site name/location	Information found/connections

V. Self Check Chapter 1

Multiple Choice Questions: Choose the best answer.

1. An early childhood professional works with children from:
    A. Preschool to second grade.
    B. Age four to age eight.
    C. Birth to age eight.
    D. Birth to age six.

2. Which of the following is not one of the four dimensions of a high-quality professional?
    A. Personal characteristics.
    B. Educational degree.
    C. Professional practice.
    D. Public presentation.

3. Which of the following is the most essential emotional quality for early childhood professionals?
    A. Caring.
    B. Empathy.
    C. Compassion.
    D. Kindness.

4. Early childhood professionals must be able to:
    A. Assess learning.
    B. Collaborate with colleagues and families.
    C. Seek continued professional development.
    D. All of the above.

5. A candidate for the CDA credential must have which of the following credentials?
    A. Must be sixteen years or older.
    B. Must hold a teaching certificate.
    C. Must be able to speak, read, and write well enough to fulfill the responsibilities of a CDA.
    D. A & C only.

6. The professional practice dimension of professionalism includes which of the following?
    A. Knowledge of DAP and DCAP.
    B. Knowledge of ethical practice and ethical conduct.
    C. Knowledge of planning, assessing, reporting, reflecting and thinking.
    D. All of the above.
    E. B & C only.

7. A philosophy of education is:
    A. A set of beliefs about how children learn.
    B. A set of beliefs about how children develop.
    C. A set of beliefs about how children should be taught.
    D. A set of beliefs about how children develop and learn and what and how they should be taught.

8. Planning is an essential part of practicing the art and craft of teaching. Which of the following is not a true statement about planning?
    A. The teacher sets goals for what children will learn.
    B. The planning process has to be done only once a year.
    C. The teacher selects activities to help children achieve planning goals.
    D. To be a good teacher you must plan.

9. Advocacy is defined in many ways and includes many activities. Advocacy is defined in the text as:
    A. The process of lobbying legislators to secure services for children and families.
    B. The act of promoting the causes of children and families to the profession and the public.
    C. One who communicates with local, state and national leaders to enlist support for children and families.
    D. One who works with the courts to speak on behalf of children in crisis.

10. A(n) _____ refers to one who works with, cares for, and teaches children between birth and age eight.
    A. Teacher.
    B. Professional.
    C. Caregiver.
    D. Educator.

11. _____ refers to any education program for children prior to their entrance into kindergarten.
    A. Preschool.
    B. Prekindergarten.
    C. Child care.
    D. Preprimary.

12. Ethical conduct is the exercise of responsible behavior with children, families, colleagues, and community members. Ethical practice is a component of which of the following dimensions of professionalism?
    A. Personal characteristics.
    B. Educational attainment.
    C. Professional practice.
    D. Public presentation.

Discussion Questions

1. Early childhood professionals work with children and families every day. The early childhood professional must know about and demonstrate essential knowledge of the profession and professional practice. According to the text, what is included in this essential knowledge?

2. Linda Luna DeMino, 2001 Texas Teacher of the Year, discusses her philosophy of education and in her philosophy she identifies a formula for success. Explain the formula for success and identify the dimensions of professionalism that support the formula.

3. Identify and discuss the important elements of professional practice.

CHAPTER 2

EARLY CHILDHOOD EDUCATION TODAY: UNDERSTANDING CURRENT ISSUES

I.   Chapter Objectives

Learner outcomes:
The learner will:

- describe the critical issues facing children and families today;

- explain how social, political, economic and educational issues influence and change child rearing, early childhood education, and teaching;

- explore the implications contemporary issues have for curriculum, teaching and life outcomes of children and families.

II.   Chapter Overview

What critical issues do children, families, and early childhood professionals face today?

How do contemporary issues influence curriculum, teaching, and the life outcomes of children and families?

How can early childhood professionals respond to contemporary social problems for the betterment of children and families?

What are some ways you can keep current in the rapidly changing field of early childhood education?

III. Chapter 2 Study Guide
Text pages 28-55.

Directions: As you read the chapter, answer the following questions. Use the guide to study the chapter information.

Issues Influencing the Practice of Early Childhood Education

1. Issues facing children and families today are in the news daily. The nation's interest is focused on young children and their families. Read the headlines in Figure 2.1. Watch your newspapers for headlines that call attention to young children and families. List below the information you find in your local paper.

_____

_____

_____

_____

_____

_____

2. Identify the ways that families changed in the twentieth century.

    Structure

    _____

    _____

    _____

    _____

    Roles

    _____

    _____

    _____

    _____

Responsibilities

_____

_____

_____

_____

_____

3.   Early childhood professionals agree that the best way to meet the needs of children and families is through their families. List the four reasons given for working with children through their family system.

_____

_____

_____

_____

_____

4.   Many issues impact families and early childhood professionals. Review the issues below to help you better understand how they affect children, families and the early childhood professional.

Working parents_____

_____

_____

_____

_____

Fathers_____

_____

_____

_____

Single parents_____

_____

_____

_____

_____

_____

Teenage parents_____

_____

_____

_____

_____

_____

5.   Identify the leading children's illnesses and what early childhood professionals can do to help with the problems associated with childhood illness.

_____

_____

_____

_____

_____

_____

_____

_____

_____

_____

6.   Poverty has serious negative consequences for children and families. Over four million children under the age of six live in poverty. Identify below the ways poverty is detrimental to students' achievement and life prospects.

_____

_____

_____

_____

_____

_____

_____

_____

_____

7.   Public interest in brain research has intensified over the past several years. Current brain research influences our ideas about how children learn, how to teach them. and what they should learn. What are the conclusions drawn by early childhood professionals regarding the brain research findings?

_____

_____

_____

_____

_____

_____

_____

_____

8.   Identify some of the proposals for providing violence-free homes and educational environments.

_____

_____

_____

_____

_____

_____

Politics and Early Childhood Education

9.   Politicians and politics exert a powerful influence in determining what is taught, how it is taught, to whom it is taught, and by whom it is taught. Identify the goals of Goals 2000: Educate America.

_____

_____

_____

_____

_____

_____

_____

Have the goals had an impact on the early childhood profession? Explain.

_____

_____

_____

_____

17

10. What if any progress has been made toward achieving Goal1?

_____

_____

_____

_____

_____

Federal and State Involvement in Early Childhood Programs

11. Explain why there has been an increase in federal and state funding of early childhood programs over the past decade and why the trend will continue.

_____

_____

_____

_____

_____

_____

_____

_____

12. Explain the expanded role of the federal government in the reform of public education.

_____

_____

_____

_____

_____

_____

13. Explain why support for preschool programs has shifted from private agencies to public schools.   Why are public school officials and state legislatures pressured to fund additional preschool and early education programs?

_____

_____

_____

_____

_____

_____

_____

_____

New Directions in Early Childhood Education

14. The changing needs of society cause changes in the early childhood profession. Explain the following changes that are occurring in early childhood education today that will have an influence on the early childhood profession.

Full-day, full-year services_____

_____

_____

Readiness for learning _____

_____

_____

Two-generation programs_____

_____

_____

Wrap-around services _____

_____

_____

Support for intellectual development_____

_____

_____

Early literacy learning_____

_____

_____

New curriculum initiatives_____

_____

_____

IV. Technology Tie-In

Making Connections

Explore the web sites below and find statistics related to the current status of children and families today. Subscribe to one of the e-mail newsletters to help you stay informed about current issues related to a topic of interest. Add the web sites to your Internet log that you began in Chapter 1.

The Children's Defense Fund
http://www.childrensdefensefund.org/

Center for Public Policy Priorities
http://www.cppp.org/

Connect For Kids
http://www.connectforkids.org/

V.   Self Check Chapter 2

Multiple Choice Questions: Choose the best answer.

1.   Which of the following is a contemporary social issue that affects decisions that families and early childhood professionals must make about the education and care of young children?
   A.   Problems of child abuse.
   B.   Large numbers of children and families who live in poverty.
   C.   Low-quality care and education of young children.
   D.   All of the above are issues affecting families and early childhood professionals.

2.   Families are in a continual state of change as a result of social issues and changing times. Which of the following is not a way that families changed in the twentieth century?
   A.   Structure; families now include arrangements other than the traditional nuclear family.
   B.   Numbers; families now include more children than ever before.
   C.   Roles; as families change, so do the roles that parents and other family members perform.
   D.   Responsibilities; as families change, many parents are not able to provide or cannot afford to pay for adequate and necessary care for their children.

3.   Programs that provide for the needs of children through the family system make sense for which of the following reasons?
   A.   The family has the primary responsibility for meeting many children's needs.
   B.   Professionals frequently need to address family problems and issues first in order to help children.
   C.   Early childhood professionals can do many things concurrently with children and their families that will benefit both.
   D.   A & C only.
   E.   All of the above.

4.   Fathers of today are more involved in parenting and child rearing. Which of the following is true about fathers today?
   A.   Fathers are gaining custody of their children.
   B.   There are an estimated 2 million fathers who stay home with their children.
   C.   Research is being conducted on fathers and child rearing.
   D.   All of the above are true about fathers today.

5.   Which of the following is not a true statement regarding children living in poverty?
   A.   Poor children are more likely to be retained in school.
   B.   Children in poverty are more likely than others to be "highly engaged" in school.
   C.   Poor children are more likely to become school dropouts.
   D.   Children in poverty are less likely to have parents who help their children complete homework assignments.

6. Brain research and other studies are influencing our ideas about how children learn, how to teach them and what they should learn. Which of the following is not one of the conclusions early childhood professionals have arrived at regarding young children?
   A. The period of most rapid intellectual growth occurs after age eight.
   B. It is increasingly evident that children are not born with fixed intelligences.
   C. Early experiences during critical windows of opportunity are so powerful they can change the way a person develops.
   D. Children reared in homes that are not intellectually stimulating may lag intellectually behind their counterparts raised in more stimulating environments.

7. Increasing acts of violence lead to proposals for how to provide violence-free homes and educational environments for children. Which of the following is not a proposal to help curb violence?
   A. Using the V-chip.
   B. Boycotting companies whose advertisements support programs with violent content.
   C. Teaching conflict resolution in kindergarten.
   D. A & B only.
   E. All of the above.

8. Public policies determine which of the following?
   A. The standards for curriculum in early childhood programs.
   B. Qualifications for early childhood professionals.
   C. Who is eligible for early childhood programs.
   D. B & C only.
   E. All of the above.

9. The enactment of Goals 2000 was an important political and educational event for early childhood professionals for which of the following reasons?
   A. The goals all focus on the needs of young children prior to beginning school.
   B. The goals all focus on the readiness of the young child for school.
   C. The goals have served to focus attention on the importance of the early years to future success in school.
   D. The goals established a standard system for the education of young children birth to age eight.

10. Over the past decade there has been increased federal and state funding of early childhood programs. According to the text, this trend will continue for which of the following reasons?
    A. Politicians and the public recognize that the early years are a foundation for future learning.
    B. More women are serving as leaders in federal and state government.
    C. Spending money on children in the early years is more cost effective than trying to solve problems in the teenage years.
    D. A & C only.
    E. All of the above.

11. There is a trend toward more preschool programs offered as a part of public schools. Today 42 of the 50 states offer free or subsidized preschools. Which of the following explain the increase in preschool programs?
    I.   Changing family patterns.
    II.   The rise in single-parent families.
    III. The rise in families with two adult wage earners.
    IV.   Early childhood intervention programs.

    A.   I, II, III and IV.
    B.   I, II and IV.
    C.   II and IV.
    D.   I and II.

12. The field of early childhood education is constantly changing because of the changing needs of society and families, and new research provides new directions. One of the changes is the new curriculum initiatives. Which of the following is not one of the new curriculum initiatives?
    A.   Mathematics.
    B.   Character/moral education.
    C.   Wellness/healthy living.
    D.   Early literacy.
    E.   Science education.

Discussion Questions

1. Explain the four reasons the family system approach is advocated for meeting the needs of children and families.

2. Explain why parents lobby for public support of early childhood education.

3. Describe the changes occurring in early childhood education today that will influence the practice of early childhood professionals.

CHAPTER 3

HISTORY AND THEORIES: FOUNDATIONS FOR TEACHING AND LEARNING

I. Chapter Objectives

Learner outcomes:
The learner will:

- explain the importance of the theories of great educators;

- describe the beliefs of Luther, Comenius, Locke, Rousseau, Pestalozzi, Owen, Froebel, Montessori, Dewey, Piaget, Vygotsky, Maslow, Erikson, Gardner and Hirsch;

- examine the influence of the great educators' beliefs on early childhood programs today;

- explain how theories of learning influence the teaching and practice of early childhood education.

II. Chapter Overview

Why is it important to know about the ideas, contributions, and learning theories of great education?

What are the basic beliefs of the individuals who have had the greatest influence on early childhood education?

How do the beliefs and practices of great educators influence early childhood education?

What is learning and how do theories of learning influence the teaching and practice of early childhood education?

III. **Chapter 3 Study Guide**
Text pages 56-93.

Directions: As you read the chapter, answer the following questions. Use the guide to study the chapter information.

Why Is the History of Early Childhood Education Important?

1.   List and explain three reasons why knowing about the past is important for you as an early childhood educator.

_____

_____

_____

_____

_____

_____

_____

_____

_____

2.   Define learning. Explain why theories of learning are important.

_____

_____

_____

_____

3.   Reflective practice involves three steps. List the steps and the defining questions for each step.

Step 1 _____

_____

_____

_____

Step 2 _____

_____

_____

_____

_____

_____

_____

_____

_____

_____

Step 3 _____

_____

_____

_____

_____

_____

Famous Persons and Their Influence on Early Childhood Education

4. Review the Time Line of the History of Early Childhood Education on page 68 of the text. Using the timeline, answer the following questions:

Who is called the "Father of Common Schools" and why is he called that?

_____

Who established the first kindergarten in the United States?

_____

Who opened the first public school kindergarten in the United States?

_____

26

5. Complete the table below for each notable educator and the contributions of each to early childhood education.

Historical Figures and Their Influence on Early Childhood Education

Educator	Contributions
Martin Luther	
John Amos Comenius	
John Locke	
Jean-Jacques Rousseau	
Johann Heinrich Pestalozzi	
Robert Owen	
Friedrich Wilhelm Froebel	

Jean Piaget and Constructivist Learning Theory

6.   How did Piaget view intelligence?

_____

_____

_____

_____

_____

7.   What are the basic concepts of constructivism?

_____

_____

_____

_____

_____

_____

_____

8.   According to Piaget, learning is a form of adaptation. The following terms are
        important in understanding the adaptive process. Define each term and give
        appropriate examples of each.

        Adaptation: _____

        _____

        _____

        _____

        _____

Assimilation: _____

_____

_____

_____

Accommodation: _____

_____

_____

_____

Equilibrium: _____

_____

_____

_____

Schemes: _____

_____

_____

_____

9.   What does the word conserve mean as applied to Piaget's theory?

_____

_____

_____

Give an example of conservation.

_____

_____

_____

10. Use the chart below to identify the key elements of Piaget's stages of intellectual development.

Piaget's Stages of Intellectual Development

Stage	Characteristics
Sensorimotor (birth to 2 years)	
Preoperational (2-7 years)	
Concrete operations (7-12 years)	
Formal operations (12-15 years)	

11. Complete the table below. Identify the famous researcher and briefly describe the learning theory of each person.

Learning Theories of Famous Educational Researchers

Researcher	Theory and Description
Maria Montessori	
John Dewey	
Jean Piaget	
Lev Vygotsky	
Abraham Maslow	
Erik Erikson	
Howard Gardner	
E.D. Hirsch	

12.   What is the zone of proximal development?

_____

_____

_____

_____

What is scaffolding?

_____

_____

_____

13.   List and describe the six basic needs identified in Maslow's Hierarchy of Human Needs.

_____

_____

_____

_____

_____

_____

_____

14.   Identify and describe Erikson's stages of psychosocial development in early childhood.

Stage 1 _____

_____

_____

_____

_____

Stage 2 _____

_____

_____

_____

_____

_____

Stage 3 _____

_____

_____

_____

_____

_____

Stage 4 _____

_____

_____

_____

_____

_____

15.   Define cultural literacy and explain the cultural literacy theory.

_____

_____

_____

_____

_____

_____

_____

16. Review Howard Gardner's theory of multiple intelligences on pages 83-85 of the text. List the nine intelligences and an example of each.

_____

_____

_____

_____

_____

_____

_____

_____

From Luther to Hirsch: Basic Concepts Essential to Good Educational Practices

17. What are nine basic concepts essential to good educational practice as they relate to children?

a._____

b._____

c._____

d._____

e._____

f._____

g._____

h._____

i._____

18. What are the basic concepts essential to good educational practice as they relate to teachers?

a._____

b._____

c._____

d._____

e._____

f._____

g._____

h._____

i._____

j._____

k._____

19. What are the basic concepts essential to good educational practice as they relate to parents?

a._____

b._____

c._____

d._____

e._____

f. _____

g. _____

IV.   <u>Technology Tie-In</u>

Making Connections

Music and the arts have had an important place in the education of young children since the beginning of the recorded history of early childhood education. Educators have supported children's involvement in music and the arts in three ways: appreciation, performance, and creation.

Visit the famous Louvre Museum in Paris at the web site below then go to the two Kid Pix sites to learn how to develop slide shows. After visiting all three sites and the sites of the four software programs listed in the text, identify how these technology tools support involvement in music and the arts. Email your journaling partner and share your conclusions about how technology can support the arts. Print a copy for your professional development notebook.

Louvre Museum Official Website
http://www.louvre.fr/louvrea.htm

Kid Pix
http://www.cap.nsw.edu.au/kidpix/kid_pix.html

Kid Pix Overview
http://www.learningspace.org/prof_growth/training/Exploratory/Kidpix/KidPixOve
rview.html

V. Self Check Chapter 3

Multiple Choice Questions: Choose the best answer.

1. Martin Luther emphasized the necessity of establishing schools to teach children to:
    A. Read.
    B. Read and write Latin.
    C. Speak Latin.
    D. Solve mathematical problems.

2. Orbis Pictus, the first picture book for children, was written by:
    A   John Locke.
    B. Robert Owen.
    C. John Amos Comenius.
    D. Martin Luther.

3. For Vygotsky, learning is supported and enhanced by others through social interaction. Which of the following is not an important concept in Vygotsky's theory?
    A. The zone of proximal development.
    B. Interpersonal interactions
    C. Scaffolding.
    D. Schemes.

4. The theory of psychosocial development is attributed to which of the following theorists?
    A. Abraham Maslow.
    B. Erik Erikson.
    C. Jean Piaget.
    D. Jean-Jacques Rousseau.

5. Friedrich Froebel's contributions to contemporary early childhood education include which of the following?
    A. The importance of learning through play.
    B. A systematic planned curriculum for young children based on songs and games.
    C. The important role of the teacher in planning the learning environment.
    D. A & C only.
    E. All of the above.

6. According to E. D. Hirsch, Jr. essentialist education includes all of the following except:
    A. A common core knowledge curriculum or "cultural currency" for all children.
    B. Children should be schooled in names, dates, places and events that are significant to our nation's past and present.
    C. A student-centered classroom.
    D. A classroom where students must learn a basic education.

7. Abraham Maslow's theory of self-actualization is based on the satisfaction of human needs. Maslow identified self-actualization as the highest human need. Which of the following is the most accurate description of the basic needs that must be satisfied for a person to reach self-actualization?
   A. Food, safety, security.
   B. Life essentials, safety and security, belongingness and love, achievement and prestige, esthetic needs.
   C. Food, safety and love, achievement and prestige.
   D. Life essentials, belongingness and achievement.

8. Howard Gardner has played an important role in helping educators rethink the concept of intelligence. Which of the following theories is attributed to Gardner?
   A. Theory of multiple intelligences.
   B. Theory of psychosocial development.
   C. Theory of cognitive development.
   D. Theory of cultural literacy.

9. In Piaget's theory of cognitive development the stages are:
   A. The same for all children.
   B. Different for atypical children.
   C. Fixed by age; the age a child goes through a stage does not vary.
   D. Varied by the sequence; each child will go through a different sequence of stages.

10. According to Piaget, children grow mentally through activity and interaction with others. Piaget believed that intelligence is the mental process by which children acquire knowledge. Which of the following processes is (are) not a part of Piaget's developmental theory?
    A. Adaptation.
    B. Scaffolding.
    C. Assimilation and accommodation.
    D. Equilibrium.

11. Many people have changed and influenced the course of early childhood education. The past influences the present and the future in education. Which of the following basic concepts is (are) essential to good education practice as it relates to children?
    A. Everyone needs to learn how to read and write.
    B. Children learn best when they use all of their senses.
    C. Social interactions with teachers and peers are a necessary part of development and learning.
    D. A & C.
    E. All of the above.

12. Which of the following is not one of Piaget's stages of cognitive development?
    A. Sensorimotor Stage, birth to 2 years.
    B. Preoperational Stage, 2 to 7 years.
    C. Conservation Stage, 7 to 12 years.
    D. Formal Operations Stage, 12 to 15 years.

Discussion Questions

1. List and discuss the reasons why it is important to know about the great educators who have influenced the field of early childhood education.

2. Identify five great educators from the past and explain their contributions to current practice in early childhood education.

3. The author identified basic concepts that are essential to good educational practices. Identify and discuss the basic concepts of good practice as they relate to teachers.

CHAPTER 4

IMPLEMENTING EARLY CHILDHOOD PROGRAMS: APPLYING THEORIES TO PRACTICE

I. Chapter Objectives

Learner outcomes:
The learner will:

- explain the importance of models of early childhood education;

- compare and contrast the basic features of early childhood education models;

- evaluate early childhood program models;

- explain how developmentally appropriate practice relates to classroom practice.

II. Chapter Overview

Why are models of early childhood education important?

What are the basic features of early childhood education models, and how are they alike and different?

What decisions do you need to make to select a particular early childhood program as a basis for your practice?

How can you apply developmentally appropriate practice to your practice of early childhood education?

III. Chapter 4 Study Guide
Text pages 94-130.

Directions: As you read the chapter, answer the following questions. Use the guide to study the chapter information.

What are Programs of Early Childhood Education?

1. What are programs for young children?

_____

_____

_____

_____

2. Today there is a demand for high-quality early childhood programs. Parents want programs that meet all of the developmental and academic needs of their children.

   What does the public want early childhood professionals to provide in early childhood programs?

_____

_____

_____

_____

_____

_____

_____

3. Child care is a comprehensive service to children and families. The major purpose of child care is to:

_____

_____

_____

_____

4. List three reasons for the popularity of child care.

    a. _____

    _____

    b. _____

    _____

    c. _____

    _____

Types of Child Care Programs

5. Briefly describe each type of child care program listed in the boxes below.

Child Care Programs

Family and Relative Care	**Family Care/Family Day Care**
Intergenerational Child Care	**Center Child Care**
Employer-Sponsored Child Care	**Proprietary Child Care**
Child Care for Children with Medical Needs	**Before- and After-School Care**

42

6. List the dimensions of quality child care and give an indicator of each.

a. _____

_____

b. _____

_____

c. _____

_____

d. _____

_____

e. _____

_____

f. _____

_____

g. _____

_____

7. High-quality early care and education have influences that last over a lifetime. What are the benefits of attending a high-quality program?

_____

_____

_____

_____

_____

_____

_____

_____

_____

High/Scope: A Constructivist Approach

8.   What are the three fundamental principles of the High/Scope model?

a. _____

_____

b. _____

_____

c. _____

_____

9.   What are the five key elements of the High/Scope approach?

Key Elements of the High/Scope Program

Key Element	Description
a.	
b.	
c.	
d.	
e.	

10.   What is the High/Scope daily routine?

Planning Time: _____

_____

_____

Key Experiences: _____

_____

_____

Work Time: _____

_____

_____

Cleanup Time: _____

_____

_____

Recall Time: _____

_____

_____

11.   Identify the advantages to implementing the High/Scope approach.

_____

_____

_____

_____

_____

_____

_____

_____

_____

Montessori Method

12.   The Montessori approach is attractive to parents and teachers today. List the reasons for the popularity of the Montessori approach.

_____

_____

_____

_____

_____

13.   The Montessori teacher demonstrates certain behaviors to implement the principles of this child-centered approach. List the teacher's six essential roles.

_____

_____

_____

_____

_____

_____

_____

14.   What are the three basic areas of child involvement in Montessori's prepared environment?

_____

_____

_____

_____

_____

15.   What are practical life activities? What is the purpose of the practical life activities?

_____

_____

_____

_____

_____

_____

_____

16.   List at least 6 sensory materials found in typical Montessori classrooms. Refer to Figure 4.5.

_____

_____

_____

_____

_____

_____

_____

17.   Explain the basic purposes of sensory materials.

_____

_____

_____

_____

18.   What is the Montessori approach to writing, reading, and mathematics?

_____

_____

_____

_____

19.   List examples of writing and reading materials used in the Montessori approach.

_____

_____

_____

_____

20.   List examples of materials for mathematics used in the Montessori approach.

_____

_____

_____

_____

_____

21.   Explain mixed-age grouping and self-pacing.

_____

_____

_____

_____

_____

22.   Review the instructional practices of the Montessori approach. Use the chart to
       record the key ideas.

Instructional Practices in the Montessori Program

Reggio Emilia

23.   What is the Reggio Emilia approach? Who founded the approach?

_____

_____

_____

_____

_____

24.   What is the theoretical base of the Reggio Emilia approach?

_____

_____

_____

_____

_____

25.   What should early childhood professionals keep in mind when considering the Reggio Emilia approach in an American setting?

a. _____

_____

b. _____

_____

c. _____

_____

26.   Using the chart below, identify the basic principles of the Reggio Emilia approach to educating young children.

Reggio Emilia Approach

Beliefs about children and how they learn.
a. Relationships b. Time

Adult's Role
a. The teacher b. The Atelierista c. Parents

The Environment
a. The physical space b. The Atelier

Program Practices
a. Documentation b. Curriculum and practices

Head Start

27.   What is the history and purpose of Head Start?

_____

_____

_____

_____

_____

_____

_____

28.   Review Head Start at a glance. How many children are served? What do you find surprising about the data?

_____

_____

_____

_____

_____

_____

29.   What are the basic principles and goals of Head Start?

_____

_____

_____

_____

_____

_____

_____

30. Use the chart below to identify and explain the services offered children and families in Head Start programs.

Head Start Services

Child Education and Development
Services to Children with Disabilities
Parent Involvement/Family Partnerships
Health Services

31. Head Start services are provided to children and families though a comprehensive child development program in Head Start-approved program options. What are the three options?

_____

_____

_____

_____

_____

32.   What is Early Head Start?

_____

_____

_____

_____

33.   All of the models described in the text have unique features but they all have the common goal of a good quality education for young children. Use the chart below to review your understanding of the models presented.

Early Childhood Education Program Models

Program	Theory	Classroom Activity	What I like about the program
Child Care			
High/Scope			
Montessori			
Reggio Emilia			
Head Start			

IV.   Technology Tie-In

Making Connections

The KinderView Internet Viewing System is another program that enables parents to check on their children during the workday. According to KinderView, the KinderView Internet Viewing System provides a unique opportunity for authorized users to view high-quality, frequently updated images of their children, completely reassured by KinderView.com's stellar security measures. Visit the KinderView site below. Read the welcome page, take a technology demonstration and read the testimonial from the parent. Reflect on the information you have about WatchMeGrow and KinderView. Identify the strengths and possible problems with an Internet viewing system. Go to the prenhall.com/morrison web site and join the chat room. Discuss your views about the Internet viewing system in the early childhood classroom.

KinderView
http://www.kinderview.com/

V.   Self Check Chapter 4

Multiple Choice Questions: Choose the best answer.

1.   The United States is once again discovering the importance of the early years. Which of the following is not one of the demands of the public?
    A.   Programs that will help ensure children's early academic and school success.
    B.   The inclusion of early literacy and reading readiness activities that will enable children to read on grade level in grades one, two and three.
    C.   Programs that exclude parents from the decision-making process in education.
    D.   Environments that will help children develop the social and behavioral skills necessary to help them lead nonviolent lives.

2.   Child care is a comprehensive service to children and families that supplements the care children receive from their families. Which of the following best describes the purpose of child care?
    A.   The major purpose of child care is to provide custodial care that meets the basic needs of supervision, shelter, food and physical necessities.
    B.   The major purpose of child care is to provide education and development of the whole child.
    C.   The major purpose of child care is to provide the health, social and psychological services as needed.
    D.   The major purpose of child care is to facilitate optimum development of the whole child and support efforts to achieve this goal.
    E.   None of the above.

3.   When child care is provided in a child's own family or in a family-like setting it is known as:
    A.   Family Day Care.
    B.   Intergenerational Care.
    C.   Proprietary Child Care.
    D.   Family and Relative Care.
    E.   None of the above.

4.   High-quality early care and education have influences that last over a lifetime. Children who attend high-quality programs experience all of the following except:
    I.   Higher cognitive test scores than other children from toddler years to age twenty-one.
    II.   Higher academic achievement in both reading and math.
    III.   Better scores in math ability than children in low-quality care.
    IV.   More years of education completed and greater likelihood of attending a four-year college or university.

    A.   I, II and IV.
    B.   I, III and IV.
    C.   II, III and IV.
    D.   I and IV only.
    E.   I, II, III and IV.

5. There are many options for child care. Regardless of the kinds of child care provided, what are the three issues identified in the text that are always a part of the child care landscape?
   A. Education, affordability and accessibility.
   B. Quality, affordability and accessibility.
   C. Quality, education and affordability.
   D. Affordability, accessibility and services.

6. The High/Scope educational approach is based on Piaget's cognitive development theory. Which of the following is not one of the three fundamental principles of High/Scope?
   A. Active participation of children in choosing and evaluating learning activities.
   B. Regular daily planning.
   C. Regular daily testing to assess progress toward program goals.
   D. Developmentally sequenced goals and materials for children based on "key experiences."

7. Professionals who use the High/Scope curriculum must create a context for learning by implementing and supporting five essential elements. Which of the following is not one of the five essential elements of the High/Scope approach?
   A. Classroom arrangement.
   B. Passive learning.
   C. The daily schedule.
   D. Assessment.
   E. The curriculum content.

8. Montessori programs are popular with parents. Which of the following is not a reason for the popularity of the Montessori approach?
   A. Montessori education has always been identified as quality education for young children.
   B. Montessori programs are not available in public schools.
   C. Parents who observe a good Montessori program like the orderliness and calm environment of the program.
   D. In Montessori programs the child is at the center of the learning process.

9. The prepared environment emphasizes practical activities such as carrying trays and chairs, greeting a visitor and learning self-care skills. These activities include polishing mirrors, sweeping floors, and dusting furniture. Montessori believed that:
   A. Children need to know how to clean up the classroom.
   B. Teachers should tell children exactly how to do the sweeping and dusting so they will know how to complete the task successfully.
   C. Involvement and concentration in motor activities help make the child independent of the adult and develop concentration.
   D. Children should be made to polish shoes or scrub tables for at least twenty minutes in order to clean them properly.

10. Reggio Emilia, a city in northern Italy, is widely known for its approach to educating young children. All of the following are beliefs of the Reggio schools about children and how they learn except:
    A. Just as Vygotsky believed, individualism is valued over relationships.
    B. Time is not set by a clock or a calendar but by the children's own sense of time and their personal rhythm.
    C. Parents have the right to be involved in the life of the school, and teachers have the right to grow professionally.
    D. Teachers must observe and listen closely to children to know how to plan or proceed with their work.

11. Head Start was implemented in 1965 and has grown in size and effectiveness. The purpose of Head Start is:
    A. To give all children a "head start" in kindergarten.
    B. To give all children who speak English as a second language a "head start" on their public school experience.
    C. To give all children from low-income families a "head start" for learning and to promote success in school and life.
    D. To give children who did not do well in kindergarten a "head start" on their first grade experience.

12. Head Start is based on the premise that all children have basic physical, social, emotional, and cognitive needs and that children of low-income families in particular can benefit from a comprehensive developmental program to meet these needs. Which of the following are goals of Head Start?
    A. The improvement of the child's health and physical abilities.
    B. The encouragement of self-confidence and self-discipline.
    C. An increase in the ability of children and their families to relate to each other and to others in a loving and supporting manner.
    D. A & B only.
    E. All of the above.

Discussion Questions

1. Discuss the benefits of high-quality care and education of young children.

2. Discuss the academic component of Montessori's approach to learning, including reading, writing and mathematics.

3. Discuss the Reggio Emilia approach to early education and the differences one must keep in mind when considering this approach in an American early care and education setting.

CHAPTER 5

OBSERVING AND ASSESSING YOUNG CHILDREN: GUIDING, TEACHING, AND LEARNING

I. Chapter Objectives

Learner outcomes:
The learner will:

- describe the role of assessment in early childhood programs;

- explain the purposes of observation and assessment;

- analyze various methods of assessing development, learning and behavior;

- determine the ethical and developmental guidelines for various assessment strategies.

II. Chapter Overview

Why is it important for early childhood educators to know how to assess?

What are the purposes and uses of observation and assessment?

What are some ways you can assess children's development, learning, and behavior?

How can I ensure that my assessment and observation is developmentally appropriate and adheres to the ethics of the profession?

III. Chapter 5 Study Guide
Text pages 132-156.

Directions: As you read the chapter, answer the following questions. Use the guide to study the chapter information.

What is Assessment?

1. Define assessment. Why is assessment important?

_____

_____

_____

_____

_____

_____

2. Identify the purposes of assessment for each of the following groups:

For Children

_____

_____

_____

_____

For Families

_____

_____

_____

_____

_____

For Early Childhood Programs

_____

_____

_____

_____

_____

Early Childhood Teachers

_____

_____

_____

_____

_____

The Public

_____

_____

_____

_____

3.   Define authentic assessment.

_____

_____

_____

_____

4.   What are the characteristics of authentic assessment?

a. _____

b. _____

c. _____

d. _____

e. _____

f. _____

g. _____

5.   What is portfolio assessment?

_____

_____

_____

What goes in a portfolio?

_____

_____

_____

How is portfolio assessment used?

_____

_____

_____

6.   A portfolio does not include all of a child's work. Describe the criteria for including projects in a portfolio.

_____

_____

_____

_____

7.   What is the purpose of a checklist?

_____

_____

_____

8.   Describe the things a teacher should keep in mind when making and using checklists.

_____

_____

_____

_____

_____

Screening Procedures

9.   Define the term screening procedures. Explain why screening procedures are used in early childhood programs.

_____

_____

_____

_____

10.   Screening procedures can include the following:

_____

_____

_____

_____

_____

11. Screening instruments provide information for grouping and planning instructional strategies. Describe the following screening instruments and give the purpose of each.

Brigance ® K and 1 Screen

_____

_____

_____

_____

_____

Dial-3

_____

_____

_____

_____

12. Define the following:

Formal assessment

_____

_____

Informal screening

_____

_____

Using Observation to Assess

13. _____ is the intentional, _____ act of

looking at the _____ of a child or children in a particular setting,

program, or situation. Observation is _____ (formal or informal)

assessment.

14.   What is "kidwatching"?

_____

_____

_____

15.   What are the purposes of observation?

a.   _____

b.   _____

c.   _____

d.   _____

e.   _____

f.   _____

g.   _____

16.   What are the advantages of systematic observation?

a.	b.	c.
d.	e.	f.

17.   Review the process of observation. Complete the chart below.

Steps for Conducting Observations

Step 1 _____	
Step 2 _____	
Step 3 _____	
Step 4 _____	

Reporting to and Communicating with Parents

18.   Reporting to parents is an important responsibility of the early childhood
       professional. Identify the guidelines for reporting assessment information to
       parents.

       a. _____

       _____

       b. _____

       _____

       c. _____

       _____

What Are the Issues in the Assessment of Young Children?

19.   Explain the following assessment issues and describe the implications for early childhood professionals.

Assessment and Accountability _____

_____

_____

_____

_____

_____

_____

High-Stakes Testing _____

_____

_____

_____

_____

_____

_____

_____

At-Home Testing _____

_____

_____

_____

_____

IV. Technology Tie-In

Making Connections

Portfolio assessment and work samples are informal methods of assessment discussed in the text. They are labeled as informal because they do not entail standard guidelines for administration and use. Go to the web site below and review the Work Sampling System. Be sure to explore the examples and the descriptions of all parts of the system. Review the purposes of assessment in Figure 5.1 on page 135 and the guidelines for reporting to parents on page 152. Create a chart that shows how portfolios, work samples and checklists help teachers meet the purposes of assessment and enable teachers to effectively communicate with parents.

Work Sampling in the Classroom
http://www.pearsonearlylearning.com/index2.html

V. Self Check Chapter 5

Multiple Choice Questions: Choose the best answer.

1. Authentic assessment has all of the following characteristics except:
    A. A paper and pencil test designed by the teacher to test what has been taught in a lesson.
    B. It assesses children on the basis of their actual work.
    C. It provides for ongoing assessment over the entire school year.
    D. It takes into account children's cultural, language, and other specific needs.

2. The _____ is an instrument designed for screening large numbers of prekindergarten children on the development of motor skills, concepts, and language skills.
    A. Brigance® K and 1 Screen.
    B. Dial-3.
    C. High/Scope Child Observation Record.
    D. Portfolios.

3. The _____ is an evaluation instrument designed to evaluate skills such as color recognition and the ability to follow directions.
    A. Brigance® K and 1 Screen.
    B. Dial-3.
    C. High/Scope Child Observation Record.
    D. Portfolios.

4. Observations are designed to gather information on which to base decisions, make recommendations, develop curriculum and plan activities and learning strategies. The purposes of observation include:
    A. To determine the cognitive, linguistic, social, emotional, and physical development of children.
    B. To identify children's interests and learning styles.
    C. To provide information to parents.
    D. A & C only.
    E. All of the above.

5. Today there is a tremendous emphasis on testing and the use of standardized tests to measure achievement. This emphasis will continue for all of the following reasons except:
    A. The public sees assessment as a means of making schools and teachers accountable for teaching the nation's children.
    B. Assessment is seen as playing a critical role in improving education.
    C. Assessment results are seen as a way to make sure that children learn and promotions are based on achievement.
    D. Professionals view standardized testing as an important way to improve their instructional practices.

6. Screening procedures give you and others a broad picture of what children know and are able to do, as well as their physical and emotional status. Screening programs for children can include which of the following?
   A. Conducting health screening, including a physical examination.
   B. Using commercial screening instruments to help make decisions regarding children's placement in programs and need for special services.
   C. Collecting and analyzing data from former programs and teachers.
   D. A & B only.
   E. All of the above.

7. All of the following are types of informal assessment except:
   A. Anecdotal record.
   B. Rating scale.
   C. Standardized test.
   D. Portfolio.
   E. Interview.

8. Checklists are a tool for observing and gathering information about a wide range of student abilities in all settings. Checklists can be used on a wide variety of topics and subjects. When making and using checklists, you should keep all of the following in mind except:
   A. Each checklist should be tailor-made for a specific situation.
   B. Make sure you are observing and recording accurately.
   C. File all checklists in students' folders for future reference and use.
   D. Use the information from checklists to create tests.

9. The purpose of the informal method for assessment and evaluation labeled _____ enables the teacher to identify children's behaviors, document performance and make decisions.
   A. Observation.
   B. Anecdotal record.
   C. Running record.
   D. Time sampling.

10. The purpose of _____ assessment is to provide documentation of a child's achievement in specific areas over time.
    A. Interview.
    B. Checklist.
    C. Portfolio.
    D. Authentic.

11. High-stakes testing occurs when standardized tests are used to make important, and often life-influencing, decisions about children. All of the following are true statements about high-stakes testing except:
    A. High-stakes tests are used to determine which children can enter programs.
    B. Generally, the early childhood profession supports high-stakes testing for children through grade three.
    C. Many politicians view high-stakes testing as a means of making sure children learn.
    D. Many administrators view high-stakes testing as a means of making sure children learn.

12. Part of your responsibility as a professional is to report to parents about the growth, development and achievement of their children. Which of the following is not one of the guidelines for reporting assessment information to parents?
   A. Be honest and realistic with parents.
   B. Communicate with parents so they can understand.
   C. Carefully word or sugarcoat the assessment data so the parent's feelings will not be hurt.
   D. Provide parents with ideas and information that will help them help their children learn.

Discussion Questions

1. Identify and explain the steps involved in the process of systematic, purposeful observation.

2. How does the early childhood professional report assessment information to parents?

3. Discuss the use of portfolios as an assessment tool. What, if any, are the problems related to the use of portfolio assessment?

CHAPTER 6

INFANTS AND TODDLERS: FOUNDATIONAL YEARS FOR LEARNING

I.   Chapter Objectives

Learner outcomes:
The learner will:

- analyze the influence of brain research on the care and education of infants and toddlers;

- describe the cognitive, language, and social milestones of infant and toddler development;

- explain the connection between infant and toddler development and developmentally appropriate practice;

- apply quality standards for infants and toddlers to program development.

II.   Chapter Overview

How is brain research influencing the care and education of infants and toddlers?

What are the cognitive, language, and social milestones of infant and toddler development?

How can I use knowledge of infant and toddler development to guide my developmentally appropriate practice?

How can I provide quality programs for infants and toddlers?

III. Chapter 6 Study Guide
Text pages 158-187.

Directions: As you read the chapter, answer the following questions. Use the guide to study the chapter information.

Painting Portraits of Children

1. Describe the characteristics of infants.

   _____

   _____

   _____

   _____

   _____

   _____

   _____

2. Describe the characteristics of toddlers.

   _____

   _____

   _____

   _____

   _____

   _____

   _____

What Are Infants and Toddlers Like?

3. Complete the following statements.

   Infancy is from _____ to _____ and includes

   _____

   _____.

Toddlerhood is the period between _____and _____ years.

Two of the most outstanding developmental milestones of infants and toddlers are

_____ and rapid _____ development.

Young Brains: A Primer

4.   Complete the following statements to identify facts about the brain.

The young brain is like the adult brain, except it is _____.

The average adult brain weights approximately _____ pounds.

At birth, the infant's brain weighs _____; at six months, _____; and at

two years, _____.

At birth the brain has _____neurons.

Shearing or pruning is _____

_____.

Synapses are _____.

Critical periods are _____

_____.

5.   What are the implications of brain research for early childhood practice?

_____

_____

_____

_____

_____

_____

_____

_____

Nature, Nurture, and Development

6. Explain the nature vs. nurture debate.

_____

_____

_____

_____

_____

_____

_____

_____

_____

Motor Development

7. What are the basic principles that govern human motor development?

a. _____

_____

_____

b. _____

_____

_____

c. _____

_____

_____

d. _____

_____

_____

Intellectual Development

8.   Using the discussion on pages 171-174 and Table 6.3, construct a chart recording the major points in Piaget's sensorimotor stages of cognitive development.

Piaget's Sensorimotor Stages of Cognitive Development

Stage	Age	Behavior
1.		
2.		
3.		
4.		
5.		
6.		

9.   Refer to Figure 6.7, page 174. Identify the characteristics of enriched environments for young children.

_____

_____

_____

_____

_____

_____

_____

_____

Language Development

10.   Discuss the role of heredity in language development.

_____

_____

_____

_____

_____

_____

11.   Discuss Eric Lenneberg's theory about language acquisition.

_____

_____

_____

_____

_____

12.   Identify and discuss the two sensitive periods of language development
       described by Montessori.

       a. _____

       _____

       b. _____

       _____

13.   Discuss the role of environment in language development.

_____

_____

_____

_____

14. Children develop language in predictable sequences. Identify each of the following sequences in language acquisition.

Sequence of Language Acquisition

First Words

Holophrasic Speech

Symbolic Representation

Vocabulary Development

Telegraphic Speech

Motherese or Parentese

Negatives

15. Refer to Figure 6.9, page 180. What are some of the important guidelines that will help promote children's language development?

_____

_____

_____

_____

_____

_____

_____

Developmentally Appropriate Infant and Toddler Programs

16. NAEYC defines developmentally appropriate as having the following three dimensions:

a. _____

b. _____

c. _____

17. Programs for infants and toddlers are based on the dimensions of developmentally appropriate practice, but professionals must also provide different programs of activities for infants and toddlers. What must early childhood professionals do to design appropriate programs for infants and toddlers?

_____

_____

_____

_____

_____

_____

Multiculturally Appropriate Practice

18.   Children and families come from culturally diverse backgrounds. It is important for
       teachers and caregivers to get to know their children and families and to be culturally
       sensitive in their care and education practices. What are the guidelines for
       multicultural practice with infants and toddlers?

       _____

       _____

       _____

       _____

       _____

       _____

       _____

       _____

       _____

Curricula for Infants and Toddlers

19.   Curricula for infants and toddlers consist of all the activities and experiences they
       are involved in while under the direction of professionals. Curriculum planning for
       infants and toddlers includes the following concepts:

       _____

       _____

       _____

       _____

       _____

       _____

       _____

       _____

       _____

IV. Technology Tie-In

Making Connections

Go to the Zero to Three web site. Read the article titled "There is No Myth". Reflect on the article. Journal with your partner. Be prepared to discuss the information in class. Print the article and place it in your professional development notebook.

No Myth of the First Three Years
http://www.zerotothree.org/no-myth.html

V.   Self Check Chapter 6

Multiple Choice Questions: Choose the best answer.

1.   All children are different and unique. Development follows an approximate range of ages. Which of the following characteristics is not a description of a behavior typical of an infant 0–12 months old?
      A.   Sits with support.
      B.   Can discriminate among sweet, bitter, and salty.
      C.   Loves to interact with others, more aware of self and others.
      D.   Mimics adults' facial expressions and gestures.

2.   Brain and child development research have several implications for those who care for young children. Which of the following is not a key factor for early childhood professionals to know?
      A.   Babies are born to learn.
      B.   Remediation is more beneficial than prevention and early intervention strategies.
      C.   What happens to babies early in life has a long-lasting influence on how children develop and learn.
      D.   Critical periods influence learning positively and negatively.

3.   Human motor development is governed by certain basic principles. Which of the following is not a basic principle of motor development?
      A.   Maturation of the motor system proceeds from gross motor to fine motor behaviors.
      B.   Motor development is from cephalo-to-caudal or from head to foot.
      C.   Motor development proceeds from the distal to the proximal or from the extremities to the central part of the body.
      D.   Motor development plays a major role in social and behavioral expectations.

4.   Sensorimotor intelligence consists of six distinct periods of development. Which of the following is not one of the six periods identified by Piaget?
      A.   Coordination of primary circular reactions.
      B.   Primary circular reactions.
      C.   Secondary circular reactions.
      D.   Representational intelligence.

5.   The ability to acquire language has a biological basis but the content of the language is acquired from the environment. Which of the following statements is (are) true about a child's language acquisition?
      A.   Parents and other people are models for language.
      B.   Optimal language development depends on interactions with the best possible language models.
      C.   Development depends on talk between children and adults, and between children and children.
      D.   All are true about language acquisition.
      E.   A & B only.

6. Toddlers are skilled at using single words to name objects, to let others know what they want and to express emotions. One word, in essence, does the work of a whole sentence. These single-word sentences are called:
   A. Referential speech.
   B. Holophrases.
   C. Grammatical morphemes.
   D. Telegraphic speech.

7. Two significant developmental events occur at about age two. What are the two significant events?
   A. Symbolic representation and mental symbols.
   B. Vocabulary development and motor development.
   C. Symbolic representation and vocabulary development.
   D. Walking and talking.

8. Providing an enriched environment is a powerful way to promote infants' and toddlers' overall development. Which of the following is essential to an enriched environment for young children?
   A. Includes a wide variety of materials to support all areas of development.
   B. Enables children to learn the basic language and cognitive skills necessary for future school success.
   C. Enables children to be actively involved.
   D. Provides for children's nutritional and health needs.
   E. All of the above.

9. NAEYC defines developmentally appropriate as having all of the following dimensions except:
   A. Knowledge about child development.
   B. Knowledge of appropriate curriculum.
   C. Knowledge about the strengths, interests, and needs of each individual child in the group.
   D. Knowledge of the social and cultural contexts in which children live.

10. Curricula for infants and toddlers consist of all the activities and experiences they are involved in while under the direction of professionals. Which of the following concepts should be included in curriculum planning for infants and toddlers?
    A. Autonomy and independence.
    B. Self-help skills.
    C. Problem solving.
    D. All of the above.
    E. A & B only.

11. Early childhood professionals must get parents and other professionals to recognize that infants, as a group, are different from toddlers. Infants need programs, curricula, and environments specifically designed for them. Which of the following statements is not true about appropriate environments for infants?
    A. Infants need adults who can tolerate and allow for their emerging autonomy and independence.
    B. Infants need adults who can respond to their particular needs and developmental characteristics.
    C. Infants need especially nurturing professionals.
    D. Infants need stimulating interactions and conversations.

12.   Children and families do not all come from the same socioeconomic and cultural background, and parents do not all rear their children in the same way. Some policies or practices may conflict with some parents' cultural beliefs and practices. Which of the following questions will help you make multiculturally appropriate decisions when conflict arises?
A.   What is the cultural perspective of the family on this issue?
B.   What are some creative resolutions that address both the parents' concerns and my own?
C.   Is there any sound research data indicating that the family's practice is doing actual harm?
D.   All of the above.
E.   A & B only.

Discussion Questions

1.   List and explain the three dimensions of developmentally appropriate as defined by NAEYC. Give classroom examples of the application of each dimension.

2.   What are some facts about infant and toddler brain development? What are some of the implications these facts have for early childhood professional practice?

3.   Programs for infants and toddlers must be uniquely different from programs for older children. Identify four unique characteristics of infants and toddlers and explain the curriculum implications for the early childhood professional.

CHAPTER 7

THE PRESCHOOL YEARS: GETTING READY FOR SCHOOL

I.   Chapter Objectives

Learner outcomes:
The learner will:

- explain the characteristics of preschool development;

- describe how play promotes children's learning;

- identify the issues and changes facing preschool programs today;

- apply developmentally appropriate practice to the development of preschool programs.

II.   Chapter Overview

What are the characteristics of preschoolers' physical, cognitive, and language growth and development?

How does play promote children's learning?

How are preschool programs changing and what issues do they face?

How can I apply developmentally appropriate practice to my teaching of preschoolers?

III. Chapter 7 Study Guide
Text pages 188-220.

Directions: As you read the chapter, answer the following questions. Use the guide to study the chapter information.

What is Preschool?

1. Describe the characteristics of preschoolers.

_____

_____

_____

_____

_____

_____

2. Define the term preschool as used in the text.

_____

_____

_____

3. List the reasons for the current popularity of and demands for preschool programs for three- and four-year-olds:

a. _____

b. _____

c. _____

d. _____

e. _____

f. _____

4.   What are the goals of preschool education?

       a. _____

       b. _____

       c. _____

       d. _____

What Are Preschoolers Like?

5.   Describe ways today's preschoolers are different from those of previous
       generations.

       _____

       _____

       _____

       These issues raise the following imperatives for preschool teachers.

       _____

       _____

       _____

       _____

6.   The preschool child is in Piaget's preoperational stage of intellectual development.
       List the characteristics of the child in the preoperational stage.

       a. _____

       b. _____

       c. _____

       d. _____

       e. _____

7. List the ways early childhood professionals can promote children's learning during the preoperational stage of development:

a. _____

_____

b. _____

_____

c. _____

_____

d. _____

_____

e. _____

_____

f. _____

_____

8. Describe how language skills grow during the preschool years.

_____

_____

_____

_____

_____

_____

_____

_____

_____

9.   Describe the physical and motor development of the preschool child.

Physical and Motor Development of the Preschool Child

Physical Development
Motor Development

Ready to Learn: Ready for School

10.   According to the Kindergarten Teacher Survey on Student Readiness (Figure 7.5), what should preschoolers know and be able to do?

_____

_____

_____

_____

_____

_____

_____

11. Discussions about readiness have changed the public's attitude about what it means. The NAEYC position statement on school readiness states that those who are committed to promoting universal school readiness must

_____

_____

_____

_____

_____

12. Define the following important readiness skills and behaviors.

Language _____

_____

_____

_____

Independence _____

_____

_____

Impulse Control _____

_____

_____

Interpersonal Skills _____

_____

_____

Experiential Background _____

_____

_____

Physical and Mental Health   _____

_____

_____

13.   Elaborate on the following factors of readiness and culture:

All children are always ready for some kind of learning.

_____

_____

_____

_____

_____

Readiness is a function of culture.

_____

_____

_____

_____

_____

Preschool Curriculum, Goals, and State Standards

14.   The purposes for preschool are changing dramatically. Describe the trends in the preschools of today.

_____

_____

_____

_____

_____

_____

15. Quality preschools set goals in each of the following areas:

    A. Social and Interpersonal Skills

        1. _____

        2. _____

    B. Self-Help and Intrapersonal Skills

        1. _____

        2. _____

        3. _____

        4. _____

    C. Learning to Learn and Learning Readiness

        1. _____

        2. _____

        3. _____

        4. _____

        5. _____

    D. Academic

        1. _____

        2. _____

        3. _____

        4. _____

E.   Thinking Skills

   1. _____

   2. _____

F.   Language and Literacy

   1. _____

   2. _____

   3. _____

   4. _____

   5. _____

   6. _____

   7. _____

G.   Character Education

   1. _____

   2. _____

   3. _____

   4. _____

   5. _____

   6. _____

H.   Music and the Arts

    1. _____

    2. _____

    3. _____

    4. _____

    5. _____

    6. _____

I.   Wellness and Healthy Living

    1. _____

    2. _____

    3. _____

J.   Independence

    1. _____

    2. _____

    3. _____

Play in Preschool Programs

16.   _____ has traditionally been the heart of preschool programs.

Play is the process through which children _____; therefore, preschool

programs should support learning through _____.

17. Use the chart below to identify early childhood educators who valued play. List their views on play.

Early Educators and Play

Early Educator	View of Play
Froebel	
Montessori	
John Dewey	
Piaget	
Vygotsky	

18. Social play supports many important functions in the preschool classroom. Describe the four functions of play.

_____

_____

_____

_____

_____

19. Through play children learn the following:

* _____

   _____

   _____

   _____

* _____

   _____

   _____

   _____

   _____

* _____

   _____

   _____

* _____

   _____

   _____

* _____

   _____

   _____

* _____

   _____

   _____

   _____

20.   Using the box below, describe each of Mildred Parten's types of social play.

Mildred Parten's Types of Social Play

Unoccupied play	
Solitary play	
Onlooker play	
Parallel play	
Associative play	
Cooperative play	

21. In addition to social play, there are other types of play. Describe the various types of play and their benefits below.

Cognitive play

_____

_____

Functional play

_____

_____

Symbolic play

_____

_____

Playing game with rules

_____

_____

Informal or free play

_____

_____

Sociodramatic play

_____

_____

Outdoor play

_____

_____

Rough and tumble play

_____

_____

22. What are the responsibilities of the early childhood professional in promoting a quality play curriculum?

a. _____

_____

b. _____

_____

c. _____

_____

d. _____

_____

e. _____

_____

f. _____

_____

g. _____

_____

h. _____

_____

i. _____

_____

j. _____

_____

The Preschool Daily Schedule

23.   Describe the components of a typical preschool schedule.

Preschool Daily Schedule

Opening Activities
Group Meeting/Planning
Learning Centers
Bathroom/Hand Washing
Snacks
Outdoor Activity/Play/Walking
Bathroom/Toileting
Lunch
Relaxation
Nap Time
Centers or Special Projects
Group Time

Quality Preschool Programs

24.   Parents often wonder how to select a good early childhood program. Review the
        indicators of a good quality preschool listed on pages 217-218. Rank the six you
        feel are the most important.

   a. _____

   b. _____

   c. _____

   d. _____

   e. _____

   f. _____

Successful Transitions to Kindergarten

25.   Parents and preschool professionals can help children make transitions easily and
        confidently in several ways. Review the list on page 219 and rank the six you feel
        are the most important.

   a. _____

   b. _____

   c. _____

   d. _____

   e. _____

   f. _____

The Future of Preschool Education

26.   Discuss the future of preschool education.

_____

_____

_____

_____

_____

_____

_____

IV.   Technology Tie-In

Making Connections

Interpersonal skills are important school readiness skills. Interpersonal skills include getting along and working with both peers and adults. Some critics claim that computers and other technology do not belong in early childhood programs because they interfere with the development of interpersonal skills. Go to the web site below and read the *Early Years* article "Technology and Young Children: What Parents Should Know." Reread the article "Technology in Early Childhood Programs." How do these articles support the use of computers in early childhood classrooms? Using the Acrobat format, print both articles and file in your professional development notebook for use with your parents.

EYLY: Technology and Young Children: What Parents Should Know
http://www.naeyc.org/resources/eyly/1996/09b.htm

EYLY: Technology in Early Childhood Programs
http://www.naeyc.org/resources/eyly/1996/09a.htm

V.   Self Check Chapter 7

Multiple Choice Questions: Choose the best answer.

1.   Three- and four-year-olds typically have which of the following characteristics?
    A.   Incessantly ask "why" and "how come" questions.
    B.   Base their opinions and judgments on how things look to them.
    C.   Can engage in activities that require several steps and concentration.
    D.   A & B only.
    E.   All of the above.

2.   Preschools are programs for:
    A.   Three- to five-year-old children before they enter kindergarten.
    B.   Infants to three-year-old children.
    C.   Prekindergarten children.
    D.   Toddlers.

3.   Today it is common for many children to be in a school of some kind beginning as early as two or three years of age. Child care beginning at six weeks of age is commonplace for many children of working parents. Which of the following is not a true statement about early education today?
    A.   Currently about 725,000 three- to five-year-old children are in some kind of preschool program.
    B.   Forty-one states currently invest in preschool education in the form of public preschools or support for Head Start.
    C.   Since 1997, California has provided free early childhood education to every four-year-old whose parents want it.
    D.   In Georgia, preschool programs are provided for all children.

4.   Preschools today have changed. Which of the following is no longer a predominant purpose of the preschools of today?
    A.   To support and develop children's innate capacity for learning.
    B.   To deliver a full range of health, social, economic and academic services to children and families.
    C.   To solve or find solutions for pressing social problems such as preventing dropouts and stopping substance abuse and violence.
    D.   To enhance the social-emotional development of children.

5.   Preschoolers are in the preoperational stage of intellectual development. Which of the following is not a characteristic of the preoperational stage?
    A.   Children are able to conserve.
    B.   Children grow in their ability to use symbols.
    C.   Children center on one thought or idea, often to the exclusion of other thoughts.
    D.   Children are egocentric.

6. Preschools are growing in popularity. Which of the following does not help explain the current popularity of preschool programs?
   A. Many parents are frustrated and dissatisfied with efforts to find quality and affordable care for their children.
   B. More parents are in the workforce than ever before.
   C. Publicly supported and financed preschools are currently available for all students and parents interested in attending preschool.
   D. Parents, researchers and others believe intervention programs work best in the early years.

7. All children need important skills to be ready for learning and school. Which of the following skills are important "readiness" skills?
   A. Language.
   B. Experiential background.
   C. Impulse control.
   D. A & B only.
   E. All of the above.

8. Social play is important to the development of the child. Social play supports many important functions. Which of the following are important functions of social play?
   A. Play provides a context in which children learn how to compromise, resolve conflicts and continue the process of learning who they are.
   B. Social play provides a vehicle for practicing and developing literacy skills.
   C. Play helps children learn impulse control.
   D. All of the above.
   E. B & C only.

9. Early childhood teachers are the key to promoting meaningful play that promotes learning. In order to support a quality play curriculum, early childhood teachers should:
   A. Plan for specific learning activities to match the children's developmental needs.
   B. Observe children's play.
   C. Supervise and participate in children's play.
   D. All of the above.
   E. A & B only.

10. Children engage in many kinds of play. All of the following are stages of children's social play as described by Mildred Parten except:
    A. Unoccupied Play.
    B. Occupied Play.
    C. Solitary Play.
    D. Associative Play.
    E. Parallel Play.

11.   Quality preschool programs are sought after by parents. All of the following are indicators of a good quality preschool except:
       A.   Pleasant physical accommodations.
       B.   Appropriate adult-child ratio.
       C.   Quiet and teacher-supervised meal times.
       D.   Well-trained director.
       E.   Emphasis on literacy development.

12.   Language is the most important readiness skill. Children need language skills for success in school and life. One important language skill is the ability to listen to the teacher and follow directions. This important language skills is referred to as:
       A.   Receptive language.
       B.   Symbolic language.
       C.   Expressive language.
       D.   Communicative language.

Discussion Questions

1.   Readiness for life and learning begins at birth and is affected and influenced by many factors. Identify and explain the dimensions of readiness.

2.   Define the term transition. Identify ways the early childhood professional and parents can help preschool children make transitions easily and confidently.

3.   The demand for preschool education has increased just as the demand for infant and toddler care has increased. The purposes of preschool are changing dramatically. Discuss the current trend of state departments of education setting standards for preschools. How does this trend link to the issue of quality in preschool programs?

CHAPTER 8

KINDERGARTEN TODAY: MEETING ACADEMIC AND DEVELOPMENTAL NEEDS

I.   Chapter Objectives

Learner outcomes:
The learner will:

- describe how kindergarten has changed from Froebel to the present;

- examine appropriate goals, objectives, and curriculum for kindergarten programs;

- apply developmentally appropriate practice to the development of kindergarten programs.

II.   Chapter Overview

What is the history of the kindergarten and how has it changed from Froebel to the present?

What are appropriate goals, objectives, and curriculum for kindergarten programs?

How can I use knowledge of developmentally appropriate practice to help me teach kindergarten children?

III. Chapter 8 Study Guide
Text pages 222-248.

Directions: As you read the chapter, answer the following questions. Use the guide to study the chapter information.

The History of Kindergarten Education

1. _____ educational concepts and kindergarten

   program were brought to the United States in the nineteenth century.

2. _____

   established the first kindergarten in the United States in 1856 at

   _____

   The first kindergarten in the United States was based on _____

   German kindergarten concept.

3. _____

   is recognized as the main promoter of kindergarten in the United States.

   She opened her kindergarten in _____ in 1860.

4. In 1860, _____

   the toy manufacturer, attended a lecture by

   _____, became a

   convert, and began to manufacture _____

   gifts and occupations.

5. The first public kindergarten was founded in _____

   in 1873 by _____.

6. _____

   is responsible for kindergarten as we know it today.

What Are Kindergarten Children Like?

7. What are the characteristics of a kindergarten child?

    _____

    _____

    _____

    _____

    _____

    _____

    _____

8. What do children know when they enter kindergarten? Review Figure 8.2 on page 227 in the text. List the information you find most revealing.

    _____

    _____

    _____

    _____

    _____

    _____

Who Attends Kindergarten?

9. Froebel's kindergarten was for children three to seven years of age. What is the trend for kindergarten attendance in the United States?

    _____

    _____

    _____

    _____

10. Discuss the issues related to the age of admittance and compulsory attendance.

_____

_____

_____

_____

_____

_____

11. What states require kindergarten attendance?

_____

_____

_____

_____

12. The public and public schools support and provide different kinds of kindergartens. Explain the kindergarten programs and practices listed below.

Developmental Kindergarten

_____

_____

Transitional Kindergarten

_____

_____

Mixed-Age Kindergarten

_____

_____

Traditional Kindergarten

_____

_____

_____

Academic Focused Kindergarten

_____

_____

_____

13.   What is multi-age grouping? Review Figure 8.4 on page 230 in the text. Identify
        the benefits of multi-age grouping.

_____

_____

_____

_____

_____

_____

_____

Kindergarten Today

14.   Today kindergarten is in a transitional stage. Explain this statement.

_____

_____

_____

_____

15.   Use the chart below to explain the changes in kindergartens today and give the reason for the change.

Today's Changing Kindergartens

Change	Reason for Change

16.   List the 10 signs of a good kindergarten as identified by NAEYC.

_____   _____

_____   _____

_____   _____

_____   _____

_____   _____

Developmentally Appropriate Practice in the Kindergarten

17. Developmentally appropriate practice involves teaching and learning that is in accordance with children's physical, cognitive, social, linguistic, individual, and cultural development. Identify the implications of developmentally appropriate practice for kindergarten programs.

_____

_____

_____

_____

_____

_____

_____

Literacy and Kindergarten Children

18. Literacy education is an important and highly visible curriculum topic. Explain the change from reading readiness to literacy.

_____

_____

_____

_____

Why is literacy and early reading such a hot topic in kindergartens today?

_____

_____

_____

_____

19.   Refer to Figure 8.7 in the text. What are the Twelve Components of a Research-
       Based Program for Beginning Reading Instruction?

       _____

       _____

       _____

       _____

       _____

       _____

       _____

       _____

       _____

       _____

20.   Early childhood professionals place a high priority on children's literacy and
       reading success. Review the accomplishments of kindergarten children on the path
       to literacy in Figure 8.8. List the accomplishments that are most surprising to you.

       _____

       _____

       _____

       _____

       _____

       _____

       _____

       _____

21. Define the following terms used when discussing literacy instruction.

Alphabet knowledge _____

_____

Alphabetic principle _____

_____

Comprehension _____

_____

Decoding _____

_____

Onset-rime _____

_____

Orthographic awareness _____

_____

Phoneme _____

_____

Phonemic awareness _____

_____

Phonics _____

_____

Phonological awareness _____

_____

Print awareness _____

_____

22.   What do children need to know to become good and skillful readers?

_____

_____

_____

_____

_____

_____

23.   The early childhood professional is responsible for supporting the emerging reading of the young child. Refer to Figure 8.10 for suggestions for motivating children to read. Evaluate the list and select four you will implement in your classroom. Justify your choices.

_____

_____

_____

_____

_____

24.   Explain the concept of a balanced approach to reading.

_____

_____

_____

_____

_____

25.   There are several approaches to teaching reading. Identify and compare the key
        ideas of each approach listed below.

Popular Approaches to Reading Instruction

Method	Key Ideas
Sight Word Approach	
Phonics Instruction	
Language Experience Approach	
Whole Language Approach	

26. Whole language dominated early childhood practice from 1990 through 2000. Explain the controversy around this approach to literacy instruction.

_____

_____

_____

_____

_____

_____

_____

_____

Supporting Children's Attitude Toward Learning

27. Experiences children have before they come to kindergarten often influence the success of their kindergarten years. What are the three important areas of influence identified in the text?

_____

_____

_____

_____

_____

28. Research supports the importance of experiences prior to kindergarten. Identify the key ideas from the research.

_____

_____

_____

_____

_____

29.   Discuss the key findings from The Early Childhood Longitudinal Study,
      Kindergarten Class of 1998-1999, sponsored by the U.S. Department of
      Education. What are the implications of this study on our practice in kindergarten
      classrooms?

      Findings

      _____

      _____

      _____

      _____

      _____

      Implications for practice

      _____

      _____

      _____

      _____

      _____

      _____

      _____

IV.   Technology Tie-In

Making Connections

Using talking books in the classroom allows children to hear and see print as they
follow along with the book. Review "Twelve Things You Can Do with Talking
Books in a Computer Center" on pages 238-239 of the text. Go to the web site
below and search for talking books for children. Locate 5 books and make a list of
the titles, publishers, and sources. Compare your findings with others in your
class.

Ask Jeeves
http://www.askjeeves.com

V.   Self Check Chapter 8

Multiple Choice Questions: Choose the best answer.

1.   The first kindergartens in the United States were based on _____'s theory of kindergarten education.
   A.   Montessori.
   B.   Froebel.
   C.   Dewey.
   D.   Piaget.

2.   The person most responsible for kindergarten as we know it today is:
   A.   Mary Mann.
   B.   Elizabeth Peabody.
   C.   Patty Smith Hill.
   D.   Susan Blow.

3.   Kindergarten children are like other children in some ways yet they have characteristics that make them unique individuals. All of the following are characteristics of kindergarten children except:
   A.   Socially, kindergarten children prefer to work in cooperative groups.
   B.   Most kindergarten children are very confident and eager to accept responsibility.
   C.   Kindergarten children are in a period of rapid intellectual and language growth.
   D.   Kindergarten children are energetic.

4.   Mixed age or multiage grouping provides an approach to meeting the individual and collective needs of children. Which of the following is not a benefit of multiage grouping?
   A.   In a multiage classroom, children have a broader range of children to associate with than they would in a same-age classroom, giving them more opportunities for diverse social interactions.
   B.   Multiage grouping provides teachers an opportunity to grow professionally by changing their grade-level assignments every year.
   C.   Mixed age grouping provides for a continuous progression of learning.
   D.   Mixed age grouping provides materials and activities for a wider range of children's abilities and allows for a continuous progression of learning.

5.   Literacy has replaced reading readiness as the main objective of many kindergarten and primary programs. Literacy means the ability to:
   A.   Read and write.
   B.   Recognize letters and their phonemic sounds.
   C.   Read, write, speak and listen, with emphasis on learning to read and write well.
   D.   Read, write and communicate verbally within the context of one's cultural and social setting.

6. Literacy is a highly visible topic today. Many state governments are mandating literacy initiatives. Which of the following are identified in the twelve essential components of a research-based program for beginning reading instruction identified in the Texas Reading Initiative?
   A. Children have opportunities to expand their use and appreciation of oral language.
   B. Systematic, direct reading instruction begins in the first grade.
   C. Children have opportunities to read and comprehend a wide assortment of books and other texts.
   D. All of the above.
   E. A & C only.

7. Children need to have many skills to become good readers. Research identifies which of the following skills as important for good readers?
   A. Knowledge of letter names and phonemic awareness.
   B. Speed in naming individual letters and experience with books and being read to.
   C. Experience with books and being read to.
   D. A & B.
   E. A & C.

8. _____ is the ability to deal explicitly and segmentally with sound units smaller than the syllable.
   A. Alphabetic principle.
   B. Phonological awareness.
   C. Phonemic awareness.
   D. Phonics.

9. Literacy and reading are important national and educational goals for young children and for everyone. How best to promote literacy has always been a controversial topic. The approach to literacy and reading that follows the philosophy of progressive education, is child centered, links oral and written language and maintains that literacy education should be meaningful to children is called the:
   A. Sight word approach.
   B. Phonics approach.
   C. Whole language approach.
   D. Language experience approach.
   E. None of the above.

10. The transition from home to preschool to kindergarten influences positively or negatively children's attitudes toward learning. Which of the following statements regarding success in kindergarten is supported by the research reported in the text?
   A. Children whose parents expect them to do well in kindergarten and who have teachers with high expectations do better than children whose parents have low expectations for them.
   B. Children with less preschool experience have fewer adjustments to make than those who have been in school from a very early age.
   C. Developmentally appropriate classrooms and practices have no effect on a child's success in learning.
   D. Rejected children have no more difficulty with school tasks than other children.

11. Despite our intuitive feelings that children who are redshirted or retained will be more successful in school, research unequivocally refutes that assumption. Research reports all of the following about children who are redshirted except:

A. They are primarily boys with birth dates immediately before the entrance cutoff.

B. They are more likely to receive special education services than their peers who enter on time.

C. The achievement of redshirts is comparable to their normally entered peers.

D. The achievement of redshirts exceeds their grade-level peers who had summer birthdays but entered school on time.

12. A _____ to reading is an approach that includes whole language methods and phonics instruction and meets the specific needs of individual children.

A. Combined approach.

B. Balanced approach.

C. Basal approach.

D. Direct approach.

Discussion Questions

1. What are the ten signs of a good kindergarten identified by NAEYC?

2. What are kindergarten children like?

3. Discuss the controversy over appropriate literacy instruction.

CHAPTER 9

THE PRIMARY GRADES: PREPARATION FOR LIFELONG SUCCESS

I. Chapter Objectives

Learner outcomes:
The learner will:

- describe the unique characteristics of the primary child;

- explain the changes in the primary curriculum;

- apply developmentally appropriate practice to teaching practices in the primary grades.

II. Chapter Overview

What are the unique physical, cognitive, language, and psychosocial characteristics of primary children?

How is the curriculum of the primary grades changing?

How can I apply developmentally appropriate practice to my teaching in the primary grades?

III. Chapter 9 Study Guide
Text pages 250-278.

Directions: As you read the chapter, answer the following questions. Use the guide to study the chapter information.

Primary Children: Growth and Development

1. Describe the portrait of a primary child.

    _____

    _____

    _____

    _____

    _____

    _____

    _____

    _____

2. Identify the unique characteristics of primary age children in each of the areas listed.

Characteristics of Primary Children

Physical development
Motor development
Cognitive development

3.   Explain the following theories of moral development as they relate to the primary years.

Jean Piaget

_____

_____

_____

_____

_____

Lawrence Kohlberg

_____

_____

_____

_____

_____

4.   Piaget's and Kohlberg's theories of moral development have implications for the classroom. Identify the classroom practices described in the text.

_____

_____

_____

_____

_____

_____

_____

The Contemporary Primary School

5.   Define integrated curriculum. Identify the theories that support integrated curriculum and explain why this approach is advocated for primary education.

_____

_____

_____

_____

_____

_____

6.   Identify the critical features of an effective primary classroom designed to help children learn in today's demanding educational environment.

_____

_____

_____

_____

_____

_____

_____

_____

_____

7.   What is pro-social behavior?

_____

_____

_____

_____

8. Identify at least six things educators can do to foster development of pro-social skills in the classroom.

a. _____

b. _____

c. _____

d. _____

e. _____

f. _____

9. What is character education?

_____

_____

_____

_____

_____

_____

_____

10. Identify at least five important character traits commonly included in the curriculum of the primary grades.

a. _____

b. _____

c. _____

d. _____

e. _____

11. Examine Bloom's hierarchy of questioning levels. List the levels and create one question for each level.

_____

_____

_____

_____

_____

_____

_____

12. Thinking skills are now included in classroom instruction. In classrooms that emphasize thinking, students are encouraged to use their power of analysis and teachers ask higher-level open-ended questions to promote thinking. Define each of the commonly taught thinking skills listed below.

a. Analyzing _____

_____

b. Inferring _____

_____

c. Comparing and contrasting _____

_____

d. Predicting _____

_____

e. Hypothesizing _____

_____

f. Critical thinking _____

_____

g. Reasoning deductively _____

_____

h. Reasoning inductively _____

_____

i. Organizing _____

_____

j. Classifying _____

_____

k. Making decisions _____

_____

l. Solving problems _____

_____

13. What are the guidelines for promoting thinking in the primary classroom?

_____

_____

_____

_____

_____

_____

_____

14. Today there is an emphasis in all levels of education to devise ways to help students apply what they learn in school to real life and real careers. What is School-to-Work? What are work-related skills?

_____

_____

_____

_____

_____

_____

_____

15. Today's primary classrooms emphasize literacy development and reading. Refer to the Florida standards for reading in grades 1, 2 and 3 in Figure 9.6 on pages 269-271 of the text. Complete the chart below citing the differences in the requirements across the primary years.

Florida Reading Standards

Grade 1	Grade 2	Grade 3

16. Mathematics is being reemphasized as an essential part of primary education. What is the difference between the "old" math and the "new-new math"?

_____

_____

_____

_____

_____

_____

17. The National Council of Teachers of Mathematics identified ten understandings and competencies for math education. Identify the ten below.

_____

_____

_____

_____

_____

_____

_____

_____

_____

18. Review the California Standards for Math in Grades 1, 2 and 3 in Figure 9.7 on pages 272-273 of the text. Identify the categories for math instruction. Review each grade level. What changes do you see in requirements by third grade?

_____

_____

_____

_____

_____

_____

_____

_____

19. Retention is a popular solution for poor achievement but research does not support retention as a solution to the problem. Identify at least six of the strategies that help improve student achievement and tell how the strategy will help students who are struggling.

_____

_____

_____

_____

_____

_____

_____

_____

20. What is looping? What are some advantages of looping?

_____

_____

_____

_____

_____

21. What is a nongraded classroom? What are some advantages of a nongraded classroom?

_____

_____

_____

_____

_____

22. In the future, the primary grades will continue to have a strong emphasis on academics, higher achievement, and helping students be successful. What are some things teachers can do to create classrooms that support children's learning?

_____

_____

_____

_____

_____

_____

_____

_____

IV. <u>Technology Tie-In</u>

Making Connections

Portfolios have long been used in early childhood classrooms to document student learning. Electronic portfolios are great student motivators, and they provide an answer to the question – How do I store all the "stuff"? One type of multimedia software that can be used to develop electronic portfolios is HyperStudio. Go to the web sites below and learn more about HyperStudio. See if you can develop a HyperStudio stack after working through the tutorial.

On-line Technology Practice Modules-HyperStudio
http://www.internet4classrooms.com/on-line_hyperstudio.htm

On-line Technology Tutorials from Around the World Wide Web
http://www.internet4classrooms.com/on-line2.htm#hs

V. Self Check Chapter 9

Multiple Choice Questions: Choose the best answer.

1. A major difference between the thinking of the preschooler and the primary age child is:
   A. The thinking of the primary age child has become more abstract and concrete objects are no longer required.
   B. The thinking of the primary age child has become motor-bound rather than perception-bound.
   C. The thinking of the primary age child has become less egocentric and more logical.
   D. The thinking of the primary age child has become more egocentric and less logical.

2. Which of the following statements best describes the behavior of a child in Stage 2 of Kohlberg's Preconventional Stage of moral development?
   A. The exchange of viewpoints with others helps determine what is good or bad.
   B. Children operate within and respond to physical consequences of behavior.
   C. Concepts of right and wrong are determined by judgments of adults.
   D. Children's actions are motivated by satisfaction of needs.

3. A nearly universal characteristic of primary children (ages 6–8) is:
   A. They are in a state of almost constant physical activity.
   B. Girls' motor skills during this period are more advanced than those of boys.
   C. They are no longer eager to learn.
   D. They prefer to work alone.

4. Reform is sweeping across the educational landscape. Schooling in the primary years has become a serious enterprise for which of the following reasons?
   A. Social and economic.
   B. Political and economic.
   C. Political, social, and economic.
   D. Political and social.

5. A lot of change has occurred in the primary grades since the 1990s. All of the following are current trends in primary education except:
   A. Single-subject teaching and learning.
   B. Integration of subject areas.
   C. Students learning together in small groups.
   D. Letter grades and report cards are still widely used but other assessment forms are used to supplement letter grades.

6. All early childhood professionals, parents, and politicians believe that efforts to reduce incidents of violence and uncivil behavior begin in the preschool and primary years. Early childhood professionals place emphasis on the following pro-social behaviors:
   A. Teaching children the fundamentals of peaceful living and cooperation.
   B. Teaching children the fundamentals of peaceful living and moral standards.
   C. Teaching children the fundamentals of kindness and helpfulness.
   D. B & C only.
   E. A & C only.

7.   Character education is rapidly becoming a part of many early childhood programs. New character education programs include which of the following?
     A.   Self-discipline, cooperation and courage.
     B.   Reasoning, respect and responsibility.
     C.   Purposefulness, perseverance and friendship.
     D.   All of the above.
     E.   B & C only.

8.   Thinking skills are used in everyday life activities to help determine the accuracy of information and to make decisions regarding choices. Commonly taught thinking skills include which of the following?
     A.   Inductive reasoning.
     B.   Deductive reasoning.
     C.   Hypothesizing.
     D.   All of the above.
     E.   A & B only.

9.   According to Bloom's taxonomy, _____ is the highest level of thinking.
     A.   Analysis.
     B.   Evaluation.
     C.   Synthesis.
     D.   Comprehension.

10. The following question clues describe the _____ level of Bloom's taxonomy: Demonstrate, calculate, compete, illustrate, show, solve, examine, change, discover.
     A.   Knowledge.
     B.   Analysis.
     C.   Application.
     D.   Comprehension.

11. Mathematics is being reemphasized as an essential part of primary education. The new emphasis on math seeks to have students be math-smart and creative users of math in life and workplace settings. Which of the following is not a strategy being emphasized in primary classrooms to support student learning of math?
     A.   Hands-on activities.
     B.   Memorization and drill.
     C.   Daily use of mathematics.
     D.   Group work and teamwork to solve problems.

12. Many politicians, educators and the public view retention as a cure for poor achievement. Research reveals that achievement-based promotion does not deal effectively with the problem of low achievement. Which of the following strategies is not a way to help with the problem of low achievement?
     A.   Use retention in kindergarten to help children with individual developmental needs.
     B.   Use after-school and summer programs to help students master skills.
     C.   Use multi-age grouping as a means of providing for a broader range of children's abilities.
     D.   Have the teacher teach the same group of children over a period of several years.
     E.   Use a nongraded classroom approach.

Discussion Questions

1. What are the characteristics of the primary child?

2. Define looping and explain the advantages of this strategy.

3. Describe the conditions that support an appropriate learning environment in the primary classroom.

CHAPTER 10

EDUCATING CHILDREN WITH DIVERSE BACKGROUNDS AND SPECIAL NEEDS: ENSURING ALL CHILDREN LEARN

I. ## Chapter Objectives

Learner outcomes:
The learner will:

- describe the concept of inclusion;

- explain how to meet the special needs of all children in a developmentally appropriate classroom;

- describe multicultural education;

- analyze strategies for infusion of multicultural content in early childhood programs and activities.

II. ## Chapter Overview

What is the basis for inclusion of children with disabilities in early childhood programs?

What is multicultural education and how can you infuse multicultural content in your programs and activities?

How can you meet the special needs of all children in developmentally appropriate ways?

III. Chapter 10 Study Guide
Text pages 280-317.

Directions: As you read the chapter, answer the following questions. Use the guide to study the chapter information.

Children with Disabilities

1. One of the most important federal laws promoting the rights and needs of children with disabilities is the

_____.

2. Review Figure 10.1, page 283 in the text. List below any new vocabulary related to children with special needs that you encounter.

_____ _____

_____ _____

_____ _____

_____ _____

_____ _____

3. What is the purpose of IDEA?

_____

_____

_____

_____

How does IDEA define children with disabilities?

_____

_____

_____

_____

4. What are the six principles established in IDEA for professionals to follow as they provide educational services to children with special needs?

a. _____

_____

b. _____

_____

c. _____

_____

d. _____

_____

e. _____

_____

f. _____

_____

5. What are the disabilities covered under IDEA?

_____   _____

_____   _____

_____   _____

_____   _____

_____   _____

_____   _____

_____   _____

_____   _____

6. IDEA mandates a free and appropriate education (FAPE) for all persons between the ages of three and twenty-one. In order to guarantee a free appropriate public education, IDEA provides federal money to state and local education agencies to support services to help support student learning. List the services specified by IDEA.

_____   _____

_____   _____

_____   _____

_____   _____

_____   _____

_____   _____

_____   _____

_____   _____

7. What is an IEP?

_____

_____

What are the purposes of the IEP?

a. _____

b. _____

c. _____

d. _____

e. _____

f. _____

g. _____

8.   What is an IFSP?

_____

_____

The IFSP provides for:

_____

_____

_____

_____

9.   What services can be provided to infants and toddlers with special needs?

_____   _____

_____   _____

_____   _____

_____   _____

_____   _____

_____   _____

_____   _____

10.   Helping parents of children with disabilities is an important role of all early
      childhood professionals. What are some strategies for involving parents of children
      with special needs?

      Administrators

_____

_____

_____

_____

_____

<u>Teachers</u>

_____

_____

_____

_____

_____

11. Define and explain the continuum of inclusive services. What are the benefits for children in inclusive classrooms?

_____

_____

_____

_____

_____

_____

_____

12. Students with ADHD generally display cognitive delays and have difficulties with learning.

Three specific areas that ADHD children experience difficulties in are:

_____   _____   _____

What is ADHD and who does it affect?

_____

_____

_____

_____

_____

What is the difference between ADD and ADHD?

_____

_____

_____

_____

13. What are the types of attention deficit hyperactivity disorder?

_____

_____

_____

14. Complete the chart below by including the characteristics of ADHD in each of the identified categories.

Characteristics of ADHD

Symptom	Characteristics
Inattention	
Impulsivity	
Hyperactivity	
Emotional Instability	

15. List at least six teaching strategies that will help you teach children with disabilities.

a. _____

_____

b. _____

_____

c. _____

_____

d. _____

_____

e. _____

_____

f. _____

_____

Gifted and Talented Children

16. What legislation was passed specifically to provide for gifted and talented children? How is gifted and talented defined?

_____

_____

_____

_____

_____

_____

_____

_____

_____

17. Early childhood professionals must challenge gifted children to think through the use of higher-order questions that encourage them to explore options and possibilities. Explain each of the seven primary ways to provide for the educational needs of gifted and talented children.

Enrichment classroom.

_____

_____

Consultant professional.

_____

_____

Resource room pullout.

_____

_____

Community mentor.

_____

_____

Independent study.

_____

_____

Special class.

_____

_____

Special schools.

_____

_____

Education for Children with Diverse Backgrounds

18.   Describe the demographic changes that will change how early childhood professionals teach and how children learn.

_____

_____

_____

_____

_____

_____

19.   Define multicultural awareness.

_____

_____

_____

_____

_____

20.   Review Figure 10.11, page 305 in the text. List below any new vocabulary related to multicultural education that you need to recall.

_____

_____

_____

_____

_____

_____

_____

_____

_____

21. Define multicultural infusion.

_____

_____

_____

_____

22. What are the guidelines to help you foster cultural awareness?

_____

_____

_____

_____

_____

_____

_____

_____

23. Selecting appropriate instructional materials to support the infusion of multicultural education is another important step in meeting the needs of the diverse learners in the classroom. Explain how each strategy contributes to the infusion of multicultural education. Give examples.

Multicultural literature

_____

_____

_____

_____

_____

_____

Themes

_____

_____

_____

_____

_____

Personal accomplishments

_____

_____

_____

_____

_____

24.   Every child has a unique learning style. What is a learning style?

_____

_____

_____

_____

_____

What are the elements of learning styles?

_____

_____

_____

_____

_____

25. Review the learning styles model developed by Rita and Kenneth Dunn in Figure 10.12 on pages 310-311 of the text. Analyze the model and identify key elements that are meaningful to you as you plan for the diverse needs of children.

_____

_____

_____

_____

_____

_____

_____

_____

26. Early childhood professionals will work with children and families from diverse cultural backgrounds. Although it is important not to generalize, there are important elements of each culture that the early childhood professional needs to know when working with children and families. Identify the key elements of the Hispanic culture discussed in the text and the implications for working with children and families.

_____

_____

_____

_____

_____

_____

_____

_____

_____

IV.   Technology Tie-In

Making Connections

IDEA defines assistive technology (AT) as "any item, piece of equipment, or product system, whether acquired commercially off the shelf, modified, or customized, that is used to increase, maintain, or improve functional capabilities of individuals with disabilities." There are a variety of software programs available that can help children with literacy development.

Go to the sites listed in Linking to Learn section in the Web Destinations module of the Companion Website – http://www.prenhall.com/morrison (two examples are given below). Search for software to assist young learners with literacy development. Go to the Tucows site below and locate the kids software section. See if you can download free software from the list in the text or a demo of software that you think will promote literacy development. What did you find? Be prepared to share your findings.

Make a list of the software you found and how it will help with the acquisition of literacy. If you found any software to download, review it and share the information on the Message Board.

Reader Rabbit's Reading Development Library, 3 & 4 – The Learning Company
http://www.learningco.com

Discis Books – Harmony Interactive
http://www.discis.com

Tucows Downloads
Tucows.com

V. Self Check Chapter 10

Multiple Choice Questions: Choose the best answer.

1. IDEA provides federal money to state and local educational agencies to help educate students in which of the following age groups?
    A. Birth to age three.
    B. From age six to age eighteen.
    C. From age eighteen to age twenty-one.
    D. All of the above are federally funded.
    E. A & B only.

2. The _____ is one of the most important educational documents in the education of children with disabilities. It constitutes a contract between the school system, the children, and the parents.
    A. LRE.
    B. FAPE.
    C. IEP.
    D. LEP.

3. The IFSP is:
    A. An individualized family service plan that specifies what services children and their families will receive.
    B. An individualized family service plan that specifies the individual education plans of the child.
    C. An initial family service plan that specifies what type of schooling the child will need when entering school.
    D. An initial family school plan that specifies when the child should enter school based on the disabling condition of the child.

4. Inclusive classrooms offer many benefits for children. In an inclusive classroom, children demonstrate which of the following?
    A. Increased acceptance and appreciation of diversity.
    B. Better communication and social skills.
    C. Greater development in moral and ethical principles.
    D. All of the above.
    E. A & B only.

5. ADHD students generally display cognitive delays and have difficulties in which of the following areas?
    A. Attention.
    B. Mental retardation.
    C. Impulse control.
    D. All of the above.
    E. A & C only.

6. The early childhood professional must plan how to create inclusive teaching environments. All of the following will help teach children with disabilities and create inclusive settings to enhance the education of all students except:
    A. Accentuate what children can do rather than what they cannot do.
    B. Use only standardized assessment so that the family will always know how the child stands in comparison to children without special needs.
    C. Use multisensory approaches to learning.
    D. Encourage parents to volunteer at school.

7. Gifted and talented children are not covered under IDEA's provisions. Professionals suggest special programs and sometimes schools for the gifted and talented. There are seven primary ways to provide for the needs of gifted and talented children. Which of the following methods of working with gifted and talented children is the most popular?
    A. Enrichment classroom.
    B. Consultant professional.
    C. Independent study.
    D. Resource room pullout.
    E. Special class.

8. One of the disabilities covered under IDEA is _____, which is defined as a communication disorder such as impaired articulation, a language impairment, or a voice impairment that adversely affects a child's educational performance.
    A. Speech or language impairment.
    B. Specific learning disability.
    C. Hearing impairment.
    D. Other health impairment.

9. Multicultural awareness is the appreciation for and understanding of people's:
    A. Cultures.
    B. Socioeconomic status.
    C. Gender.
    D. Own culture.
    E. All of the above.

10. Multicultural infusion means that multicultural education permeates the curriculum to alter or affect the way young children and teachers think about diversity issues. Infusion processes foster:
    A. Cultural awareness.
    B. Parent and community involvement.
    C. Teaching to children's learning styles.
    D. All of the above.
    E. A & B only.

11. A learning style is the way that students of every age are affected by their:
    A. Immediate environment.
    B. Own emotionality.
    C. Sociological needs.
    D. All of the above.
    E. A & B only.

12. Learning styles consist of all of the following elements except:
    A. Psychological.
    B. Sociological.
    C. Cultural.
    D. Emotional.
    E. Environmental.

Discussion Questions

1. Discuss the six principles established by IDEA for professionals to follow as they provide educational and other services to children with special needs.

2. Discuss the seven primary ways to provide for the needs of gifted and talented children.

3. Instructional materials to support the infusion of multicultural education must be carefully selected. Explain how multicultural literature, themes and personal accomplishments are utilized to enhance the multicultural materials in the classroom. Give examples of each.

CHAPTER 11

GUIDING CHILDREN'S BEHAVIOR: HELPING CHILDREN ACT THEIR BEST

I.   Chapter Objectives

Learner outcomes:
The learner will:

- explain the importance of helping children guide their own behavior;

- identify the important elements in helping children guide their own behavior;

- explain the importance of developing a philosophy of guiding children's behavior;

- plan strategies to develop the knowledge and skills necessary to successfully help children guide their behavior.

II.   Chapter Overview

Why is it important to help children guide their own behavior?

What are important elements in helping children guide their behavior?

Why is developing a philosophy of guiding children's behavior important?

What can I do now to develop the knowledge and skills to successfully help children guide their behavior?

III. Chapter 11 Study Guide
Text pages 318-341.

Directions: As you read the chapter, answer the following questions. Use the guide to study the chapter information.

How to Guide Children's Behavior

1. What does the term behavior guidance mean?

_____

_____

_____

_____

2. What are the twelve essential steps in guiding children's behavior?

Step 1 _____

_____

_____

Step 2 _____

_____

Step 3 _____

_____

Step 4 _____

_____

Step 5 _____

_____

_____

Step 6   _____

_____

Step 7   _____

_____

Step 8   _____

_____

Step 9   _____

_____

Step 10   _____

_____

Step 11   _____

_____

Step 12   _____

_____

3.   What are your basic beliefs about discipline?

_____

_____

_____

_____

4. Part of knowing children and child development is knowing and meeting their needs. Maslow's hierarchy of human needs identifies five basic needs that motivate behaviors. Explain how to apply the hierarchy to guiding children's behavior.

    a. Physical needs _____

    _____

    b. Safety and security _____

    _____

    c. Belonging and affection _____

    _____

    d. Self-esteem _____

    _____

    e. Self-actualization _____

    _____

5. Explain the term locus of control.

    _____

    _____

    _____

6. Affirming and acknowledging children's appropriate behaviors is a good way to build new behaviors. Identify below some examples of how to affirm appropriate behavior.

    Verbal

    _____

    _____

    _____

    _____

    _____

Nonverbal

_____

_____

_____

Social

_____

_____

_____

7. The role of the early childhood professional in guiding young children's behavior is to help them learn new behaviors and change or modify old behaviors. List below some ways adults can help children build new behaviors.

_____

_____

_____

_____

_____

8. Early childhood professionals need to set appropriate expectations for children. Expectations are the guideposts children use in learning to direct their own behavior. Explain the following ways of setting expectations.

Set Limits _____

_____

_____

_____

_____

Develop Classroom Rules _____

_____

_____

_____

9. Explain why it is important to set limits.

_____

_____

_____

_____

10. Environment plays a key role in children's learning and their ability to guide their own behavior.   Identify the guidelines that will help you create a classroom that supports children's guidance of their own behavior.

a. _____

_____

b. _____

_____

c. _____

_____

d. _____

_____

e. _____

_____

f. _____

_____

g. _____

_____

h. _____

_____

11. What are some characteristics of classrooms that support children as they learn how to guide their own behavior?

_____

_____

_____

_____

_____

_____

_____

_____

12. Children see and remember how other people act; therefore, it is important for the early childhood professional to model appropriate behavior. What are some important techniques for modeling appropriate behaviors?

_____

_____

_____

_____

_____

_____

13. Identify and explain the most overlooked strategy for guiding children's behavior. Explain why it is not used more frequently in guiding children's behavior.

_____

_____

_____

_____

14. Involving parents and families is a valuable way to help children learn to guide their own behavior. List some things you can do to collaborate with parents on guiding children's behaviors.

_____

_____

_____

_____

_____

15. Everyone involved in the process of education has basic rights that need to be recognized and honored. Identify some of the basic rights of each group below.

Children's Rights

_____

_____

_____

_____

_____

_____

Teachers' Rights

_____

_____

_____

_____

Parents' Rights

_____

_____

_____

_____

16. Explain the concept of classroom meetings. How do classroom meetings help foster a cooperative living and learning environment in the classroom?

_____

_____

_____

_____

_____

_____

_____

_____

17. Teaching conflict resolution strategies is important for the following reasons:

_____

_____

_____

_____

18. Strategies used to teach and model conflict resolution include:

_____

_____

_____

_____

_____

_____

_____

_____

IV. <u>Technology Tie-In</u>

Making Connections

Early childhood professionals often have children with emotional and behavioral disabilities their classrooms. Working with these children can be challenging work. Go to the web site below to learn more about KidTools. Read the profile of Matthew to learn more about emotional and behavioral disabilities. How do the twelve steps for guiding children's behavior relate to the strategies described in KidTools? What other ways can you use technology to help children manage their behavior?

Reflect on what you have learned about emotional and behavioral disabilities. Journal with your partner about the implications for technology in guiding children's behavior. Print your journal responses and file in your professional development notebook.

KidTools
http://www.coe.missouri.edu/vrcbd/projres1.shtml

V. Self Check Chapter 11

Multiple Choice Questions: Choose the best answer.

1. Guiding children's behavior is:
    A.   A process of helping children become compliant to adult rules.
    B.   A process of helping children learn to submit to the control of the authority figure.
    C.   A process of helping children learn to follow the rules.
    D.   A process of helping children build positive behaviors.

2. Children cannot behave well when adults expect too much or too little of them based on their development or when they expect them to behave in ways inappropriate for them as individuals. A key for guiding children's behavior is to:
    A.   Know what children are like by knowing child development.
    B.   Know what you believe about guidance and children.
    C.   Know what the current trends are in child guidance.
    D.   Know the guidance expectations of the family.

3. _____ felt that human growth and development was oriented toward self-actualization, the striving to realize one's potential.
    A.   Jean Piaget.
    B.   Abraham Maslow.
    C.   Howard Gardner.
    D.   Lawrence Kohlberg.

4. Early childhood professionals who are seeking to instill in children a sense of independence and responsibility for their own behavior might respond in which of the following ways to a child's efforts:
    A.   "You worked a long time building the block tower. You kept working on it until you were finished. Would you like to draw a picture of it before you take it down?"
    B.   "I like the way you built the block tower. I see you used all of the blocks I asked you to use to build the tower."
    C.   "Good job. You showed me just how perfect a tower you can build when you follow the patterns."
    D.   "Great tower. Now we don't have to be embarrassed when the towers you build fall down. When you use the new strategy I taught you, your towers will always stand tall without falling down."

5. Parents and early childhood professionals who are working to help children develop an internal locus of control will:
    A.   Give children responsibilities.
    B.   Give children choices and help them make choices.
    C.   Support children in their efforts to be successful.
    D.   All of the above.
    E.   None of the above.

6. Setting limits helps children understand what the classroom expectations are and helps define unacceptable behavior. Setting clear limits is important for all of the following reasons except:
    A. Limits provide children with security.
    B. Limits help early childhood professionals clarify what is unacceptable behavior in their classroom.
    C. Setting limits solves the problem of misbehaving children because they know what is acceptable behavior.
    D. Setting limits helps children act with confidence because they know what behaviors are acceptable.

7. Early childhood professionals create classroom environments that make appropriate behavior possible when they:
    A. Provide a place for all materials to be easily stored and put away by the children.
    B. Provide for a variety of activities both quiet and loud.
    C. Create well-defined center areas with an abundance of appropriate materials.
    D. All of the above.
    E. A & C only.

8. Telling is not teaching. Actions speak louder than words. Children see and remember how other people act. Modeling plays a major role in helping children guide their behavior. Which of the following are techniques to help children learn through modeling?
    A. Show children how and where games are stored.
    B. Have children demonstrate to other children the appropriate way to hang completed paintings.
    C. Call attention to a desired behavior when another child models it.
    D. All of the above.
    E. A & C only.

9. The Grapevine Elementary School in Texas established a discipline plan based on the desire to encourage all learners to be responsible, intrinsically motivated and self-directed. The school decided not to use rewards in their positive discipline plan. Which of the following beliefs is most directly connected to their decision not to use rewards?
    A. All human beings need to feel connected.
    B. Children can be creative decision makers and responsible citizens.
    C. All children should continuously monitor their own learning and behavior.
    D. Natural and logical consequences for poor choices encourage responsible behavior.
    E. Punishment encourages rebellion and resentment.

164

10. Which of the following strategies is considered one of the most overlooked strategies for guiding children's behavior?
    A. Modeling appropriate behavior.
    B. Ignoring inappropriate behavior.
    C. Creating a positive learning environment.
    D. Setting appropriate limits.

11. Conflicts frequently result in classrooms as a result of children's interactions with others. Early childhood professionals are increasingly teaching children ways to manage and resolve their own conflicts. Teaching conflict resolution strategies is important for all of the following reasons except:
    A. Children need the skills to resolve their own conflicts so teachers will have more time to teach the more important academic concepts.
    B. Teaching conflict resolution skills helps them use these same skills as adults.
    C. Peaceful resolution of conflicts contributes, in the long run, to peaceful homes and communities.
    D. Children who learn to resolve interpersonal behavior problems peacefully learn intuitively that peace begins with them.

12. Teachers have a responsibility to help children learn how to become well behaved and responsible. Which of the following is not one of the twelve steps in a basic approach to guiding children's behavior?
    A. Clarify your beliefs about child guidance.
    B. Know developmentally appropriate practice.
    C. Use rewards and punishments to control behavior.
    D. Establish appropriate expectations.
    E. Teach conflict management.

Discussion Questions

1. What is meant by locus of control? Explain how a classroom can support or hinder the development of an internal locus of control.

2. Explain how Maslow's hierarchy of needs relates to guiding children's behavior.

3. Discuss the concept of class meetings as implemented by the Grapevine Elementary School. Include in your discussion the key activities of the class meeting.

CHAPTER 12

COOPERATION AND COLLABORATION WITH PARENTS, FAMILIES, AND THE COMMUNITY: BUILDING A PARTNERSHIP FOR STUDENT SUCCESS

I. **Chapter Objectives**

    Learner outcomes:
    The learner will:

- explain the importance of collaboration between parents, family, and the community;

- describe the benefits of collaborating with parents, families, and the community;

- decide how you can encourage and support programs for collaboration with families and communities;

- describe effective parent/family collaboration programs.

II. **Chapter Overview**

    Why is collaboration between parents, families, and the community important?

    What are the benefits of collaborating with parents, families, and the community?

    How can you encourage and support programs for collaboration with families and communities?

    How can I conduct an effective parent/family collaboration program?

III. Chapter 12 Study Guide
Text pages 342-367.

Directions: As you read the chapter, answer the following questions. Use the guide to study the chapter information.

Redefining Parent Involvement

1.   Current accountability and reform movements have convinced families that they should no longer be kept out of their children's schools. Educators and families realize that mutual cooperation is in everyone's best interest. How have parent involvement practices changed to meet the new demands for more parental involvement?

_____

_____

_____

_____

_____

_____

2.   Discuss at least three ways that families have changed and the impact on the early childhood profession.

_____

_____

_____

_____

_____

3.   Early childhood professionals can provide support for families in a number of ways. Explain each of the following supports for families and give an example of each.

Provide support services.

_____

_____

_____

Provide child care.

_____

_____

_____

Avoid criticism.

_____

_____

_____

Adjust programs.

_____

_____

_____

Be sensitive.

_____

_____

_____

Seek training.

_____

_____

_____

Increase parent contacts.

_____

_____

_____

Parent/Family Involvement: What Is It?

4. Early childhood professionals recognize the need for family-centered teaching. List the reasons for the focus on family-centered teaching.

a. _____

_____

_____

b. _____

_____

_____

c. _____

_____

_____

5. Even Start is an example of family-centered teaching. Discuss the Even Start program and the inclusion of families in the learning process.

_____

_____

_____

_____

_____

_____

6. Explain two-generation and intergenerational family programs.

_____

_____

_____

_____

7. List the guidelines for developing programs of parent and family involvement.

a. _____

b. _____

c. _____

d. _____

e. _____

f. _____

g. _____

h. _____

i. _____

j. _____

k. _____

8. The National PTA has developed guidelines for improving family and parent involvement. What are the National PTA's standards for parent/family involvement programs?

_____

_____

_____

_____

_____

_____

_____

9.   Use the chart below to list strategies for involving families in meaningful activities
to support the school and family partnership.

Activities for Involving Families

Schoolwide Activities	Communication Activities	Educational Activities	Service Activities	Decision Activities

10.   Home visits are becoming more commonplace for many teachers today. Home
visits help teachers demonstrate their interest in children and families. Home visits
also help teachers better understand their students by seeing them in their home
environment.

Identify the guidelines for making successful home visits.

_____

_____

_____

_____

_____

_____

_____

11. Parent–professional conferences are an important tool for parent involvement. List the guidelines for parent and early childhood professional conferences.

a. _____

b. _____

c. _____

d. _____

e. _____

f. _____

g. _____

h. _____

i. _____

12. Making telephone calls is an efficient way to contact families when it is impossible to arrange a face-to-face conference. Identify the tips for successful telephone contacts with families.

_____

_____

_____

13. The Internet provides another way for you to reach out to parents and keep them involved and informed. Identify the points to consider before setting up a class web page or e-mail communication.

_____

_____

_____

_____

What is the "digital divide"?

_____

_____

_____

How does the "digital divide" affect parent/family involvement in education?

_____

_____

_____

14.   List the guidelines to follow when you communicate with parents on the Internet.

_____

_____

_____

_____

_____

_____

_____

15.   What are some practical ideas for involving single-parent families in school activities?

_____

_____

_____

_____

_____

_____

_____

16. Language-minority parents are individuals whose English proficiency is minimal and who lack a comprehensive knowledge of the norms and social systems in the United States. Discuss the issues related to involving language-minority parents in their child's education.

_____

_____

_____

_____

_____

_____

17. List the eight guidelines for culturally sensitive family involvement.

a. _____

_____

b. _____

_____

c. _____

_____

d. _____

_____

e. _____

_____

f. _____

_____

g. _____

_____

h. _____

_____

174

18. A comprehensive program of involvement is not complete without community and business involvement. Discuss the involvement of the community and business in the education of young children.

_____

_____

_____

_____

_____

What are some ways to involve the community and business in the education of young children?

_____

_____

_____

_____

_____

19. There are national organizations for family involvement in schools. Review the organizations listed in the text. Find out if there are any local chapters in your area. List below the names and contact person for any groups you find in your city or state.

_____

_____

_____

_____

20. What is the Family Involvement Partnership for Learning?

_____

_____

_____

_____

IV.   Technology Tie-In

Making Connections

Homework assignments for all children are a growing reality in many of today's primary classrooms. Homework can be a challenge for parents and children. Use the sites listed in Linking to Learn section in the Web Destinations module of the Companion Website – http://www.prenhall.com/morrison, the search engines below, or the search engine of your choice to locate information to help parents with homework. Develop an information page on homework to send home to your parents. Print any articles you find and put them in your professional development notebook.

Google
http://www.google.com

Yahoo
http://www.yahoo.com/

V.   Self Check Chapter 12

Multiple Choice Questions: Choose the best answer.

1.   Today families believe their children have a right to effective, high-quality teaching and care and have become more demanding in their quest for high-quality education. Schools are seeking ways to involve families in this quest for quality. As a result parent involvement has changed in which of the following important ways:
- A.   Schools and other agencies are expected to involve and collaborate with parents and families in significant ways.
- B.   Educators now expect that parents will be involved in the education of their children both at home and at school.
- C.   Parent involvement may mean that while teachers work with parents to help children learn they also have to teach parents how to work with their children.
- D.   All of the above.
- E.   A & C only.

2.   Early childhood professionals can help parents with their changing roles in all of the following ways except:
- A.   Provide support services to help families link up with other agencies and groups.
- B.   Provide constructive criticism when they are not spending enough time with their children.
- C.   Provide child care and seek extended services for families that need additional child care.
- D.   Adjust programs to meet the needs of the changing family.

3.   Families today are changing. There are more single-parent families and more grandparents caring for children. Which of the following guidelines were suggested to help early childhood professionals effectively involve all parents and families?
- A.   Make home visits.
- B.   Help families overcome their cultural communications preferences and learn to communicate with the method preferred by the school.
- C.   Learn how families rear children and manage their families.
- D.   All of the above.
- E.   A & C only.

4.   Collaborating with agencies such as the National PTA is an excellent way to enhance and promote your program of parent involvement. The National PTA's Standards for Parent/Family Involvement Programs help schools, communities, and parenting groups implement effective parent involvement programs. Which of the following is not an example of one of the six standards?
- A.   Parents are sent a communication informing them about decisions made that affect children and families.
- B.   Parents are invited to help with a field trip to the zoo.
- C.   The local print shop provides free printing services for all announcements of parent involvement activities.
- D.   Classroom professionals send home a parent letter every week informing parents of classroom learning and events.

5. Conducting home visits is becoming more commonplace for many teachers. Which of the following is not a true statement regarding home visits?
   A. Home visits help teachers demonstrate their interest in students' families.
   B. California pays teachers overtime for visiting students' homes.
   C. Home visits build stronger relationships with parents but do not improve attendance and achievement.
   D. Home visits help teachers understand their students better by seeing them in their home environment.

6. When conducting successful parent conferences, the early childhood professional should do all of the following except:
   A. Plan ahead.
   B. Portray an authoritative atmosphere.
   C. Communicate at parents' levels.
   D. Learn to listen.
   E. Develop an action plan.

7. Today there are many single-parent and working families. The early childhood professional should consider which of the following guidelines when involving single and working parents in school activities?
   A. Sponsor evening and weekend learning activities at which parents can participate and learn with their children.
   B. Use the "Dear Parents" greeting in letters and other messages.
   C. Welcome other children at school events.
   D. All of the above.
   E. A & C only.

8. Culturally sensitive family involvement is important for all of the following reasons except:
   A. Language-minority families often lack information about the U.S. educational system.
   B. The current educational system may be quite different from schools with which these families are familiar.
   C. Language-minority families do not value education, they value work.
   D. The demographic makeup of America is rapidly changing.
   E. Many schools have student populations in which minorities are the majority.

9. Which of the following are true statements regarding grandparents as parents?
   A. Four million children under the age of 18 are living in homes maintained by grandparents.
   B. Many of the children living with their grandparents are "skipped generation children," meaning that neither of their parents is living.
   C. Reasons for the increases in the number of children living with grandparents include drug use, incarceration and teenage pregnancy.
   D. All of the above.
   E. A & C only.

10. Activities for parent and family involvement include participation in the decision-making activities of the school. According to the text, parents should be involved in all of the following decision-making activities of a school except:
   A. Curriculum development and review.
   B. Hiring staff.
   C. Dismissal of staff.
   D. Policy making.

11. Communication is important in the school and family involvement process. All of the following are true statements about telephone contacts with families except:
   A. Telephone calls are an efficient way to contact families when it is impossible to arrange a face-to-face conference.
   B. It takes less time on the telephone to build rapport and trust.
   C. It is important to constantly clarify what you are talking about.
   D. Your telephone contact may be the major part of the family's support system.

12. The Internet provides another way for early childhood professionals to reach out to parents and keep them informed and involved. Which of the following is not one of the guidelines to follow when you communicate with parents on the Internet?
   A. Always e-mail anything that you would discuss face-to-face or in newsletters.
   B. Check with your school or program technology coordinator for guidelines and policies for communicating electronically with parents.
   C. Remember that not all parents are connected to the Internet.
   D. Observe the rules of politeness and courtesy that you would in a face-to-face conversation.
   E. Know the rules of courteous Internet conversations.

Discussion Questions

1. Identify and discuss the five areas of activities for parent and family involvement. Give examples of each.

2. Parent-teacher conferences are critical for helping families and professionals accomplish their goals for the child. Discuss the guidelines for preparing and conducting successful parent conferences.

3. There is a great "digital divide" in the United States. What is meant by the term "digital divide"? What are the implications of this problem for teaching, learning and including parents in education?

SELF CHECK ANSWER KEY BY CHAPTER

CHAPTER 1   **You and Early Childhood Education: What Does It Mean to Be a Professional?**

1.	C	11.	A	**Discussion**	
2.	B	12.	C	1.	See page 7.
3.	A			2.	See pages 16-17 and 4-19.
4.	D			3.	See pages 12-16.
5.	C				
6.	D				
7.	D				
8.	B				
9.	B				
10.	B				

CHAPTER 2   **Early Childhood Education Today: Understanding Current Issues**

1.	D	11.	A	**Discussion**	
2.	B	12.	A	1.	See pages 32-33.
3.	E			2.	See pages 51-53.
4.	D			3.	See pages 53-54.
5.	B				
6.	A				
7.	E				
8.	E				
9.	C				
10.	D				

CHAPTER 3   **History and Theories: Foundations for Teaching and Learning**

1.	A	11.	E	**Discussion**	
2.	C	12.	C	1.	See pages 58-60.
3.	D			2.	See pages 58-67.
4.	B			3.	See pages 87-89.
5.	E				
6.	C				
7.	B				
8.	A				
9.	A				
10.	B				

CHAPTER 4 — Implementing Early Childhood Programs: Applying Theories to Practice

1. C
2. D
3. A
4. E
5. B
6. C
7. B
8. B
9. C
10. A

11. C
12. E

Discussion
1. See pages 100-105.
2. See pages 112-117.
3. See pages 117-120.

CHAPTER 5 — Observing and Assessing Young Children: Guiding, Teaching, and Learning

1. A
2. B
3. A
4. E
5. D
6. E
7. C
8. D
9. A
10. C

11. B
12. C

Discussion
1. See pages 147-152.
2. See page 152.
3. See pages 136-140.

CHAPTER 6 — Infants and Toddlers: Foundational Years for Learning

1. C
2. B
3. C
4. A
5. D
6. B
7. C
8. E
9. B
10. D

11. A
12. D

Discussion
1. See pages 179-182.
2. See pages 162-165.
3. See pages 160-165&182-186.

CHAPTER 7   The Preschool Years: Getting Ready for School

1.	E
2.	A
3.	C
4.	D
5.	A
6.	C
7.	E
8.	D
9.	D
10.	B

11.	C
12.	A

Discussion
1. See pages 196-201.
2. See page 219.
3. See pages 201-204.

CHAPTER 8   Kindergarten Today: Meeting Academic and Developmental Needs

1.	B
2.	C
3.	A
4.	B
5.	C
6.	E
7.	D
8.	C
9.	D
10.	A

11.	D
12.	B

Discussion
1. See page 232.
2. See pages 224-227.
3. See pages 231-241.

CHAPTER 9   The Primary Grades: Preparation for Lifelong Success

1.	A
2.	D
3.	A
4.	C
5.	A
6.	E
7.	D
8.	D
9.	B
10.	C

11.	B
12.	A

Discussion
22. See pages 252-255.
23. See page 275.
24. See pages 274-277.

CHAPTER 10   Educating Children with Diverse Backgrounds and Special Needs: Ensuring All Children Learn

1.	D		11.	D	**Discussion**	
2.	C		12.	C	1.	See page 284.
3.	A				2.	See pages 300-301.
4.	D				3.	See pages 304-311.
5.	E					
6.	B					
7.	D					
8.	A					
9.	E					
10.	D					

CHAPTER 11   Guiding Children's Behavior: Helping Children Act Their Best

1.	D		11.	A	**Discussion**	
2.	A		12.	C	1.	See pages 327-332.
3.	B				2.	See pages 322-323.
4.	A				3.	See pages 336-338.
5.	D					
6.	C					
7.	D					
8.	D					
9.	C					
10.	B					

CHAPTER 12   Cooperation and Collaboration with Parents, Families, and the Community: Building a Partnership for Student Success

1.	D		11.	B	**Discussion**	
2.	B		12.	A	22.	See pages 354-356.
3.	E				23.	See pages 358-360.
4.	A				24.	See pages 360-361.
5.	C					
6.	B					
7.	E					
8.	C					
9.	E					
10.	C					